J. M. J.

The Holy Family Hymns

J. M. J.

The Holy Family Hymns

ISBN/EAN: 9783337278922

Printed in Europe, USA, Canada, Australia, Japan

Cover: Foto ©Thomas Meinert / pixelio.de

More available books at **www.hansebooks.com**

J. M. J.

THE
HOLY FAMILY
HYMNS.

WITH THE APPROBATION OF
HIS EMINENCE CARDINAL WISEMAN.

LONDON:
RICHARDSON AND SON,
26, PATERNOSTER ROW; 9, CAPEL STREET, DUBLIN;
AND DERBY.
1860.

London, Sept. 15, 1860.

Rev. dear Sir,

As, in addition to my official approbation, you desire to have some expression of my personal approval of this collection of Hymns for the Society of the HOLY FAMILY, I beg to assure you, that I shall welcome its publication with great satisfaction. Wishing a sincere blessing on your valuable labours,

I am ever

Your affectionate Servant in Xt.

N. CARD. WISEMAN.

FROM THE BISHOP OF SOUTHWARK.

St. George's, Aug. 28, 1860.

Many of these Hymns are suitable for the brave Catholic Soldiers of our Military Stations, and some of the Military Chaplains have expressed their delight at the prospect of the good which the using them amongst the Soldiers is likely to effect. I am glad, therefore, to think that the Rev. F. Faure intends to ask the leave of the Cardinal Archbishop to print them.

✠ THOMAS GRANT.

FROM THE VERY REV. DR. O'BRIEN, V.G.,
THE VENERABLE FOUNDER OF THE YOUNG MEN'S SOCIETIES.

Kilfinane, 31 *Aug.* 1860.

Rev. Dear Sir,

Every one who wishes well to the youth of these countries will sympathize with you in the exertions which you are making to establish congregational singing. Your success will aid the progress of civilization at the same time that it will help to embody and perpetuate the spirit of Faith and Charity in Catholic flocks. Employ my name in any way which you deem useful—I ardently hope that the Young Men's Societies will take advantage of your labours, and that I shall enjoy your Hymns and Chaunts in their halls.

I am,
Rev. Dear Sir,
Yours Faithfully,
R. B. O'BRIEN, V.G., P.P.

PREFACE.

Poetry united with Music, exercises a powerful influence on mankind—for good or evil.

In every age and country, the ministers of truth and error have endeavoured to apply this impressive power, which the world calls ' a magic spell,' to religious purposes.

All know what great influence some sects in England have acquired by their congregational singing, though a large proportion of their Hymns hardly deserve the name of music or poetry. The fact is that congregational singing brings many to strong convictions, who have long resisted other calls.

The Catholic Church has always availed herself of this powerful means of edification. She has always followed the advice of the Apostle, St. Paul (Col. iii Eph. v.,) " Teach one another in Psalms, Hymns, and Spiritual Canticles, singing in grace and making melody in your hearts to the Lord "

Hymns of Christian Doctrine have been loved and sung in the Church from the Apostles' time to our own days. Holy Popes and Doctors, Kings and pious Poets, have applied their talents to compose Hymns intended to be sung congregationally—and these Religious Hymns have ever been and are still an invaluable armoury for the defence of the Christian Faith, for the strengthening of holy love, and for the conversion of sinners.

In Germany, France, Italy and other Catholic countries the singing of religious hymns and spiritual canticles, is found among the most useful, I should even say, necessary expedients, to maintain the faith, and to convert the negligent and sinners.

Who can resist the sweet and powerful influence which

steals simultaneously over the mind, the heart, and senses?
True, it is only an aid to the grace of God, but it is an aid
which God has blest.

A consideration of the great power possessed by popular
religious singing has led the compilers, to invite many of the
Catholic Poets of England to contribute to this Hymn-book.

His Eminence Cardinal Wiseman, when consulted, gave
to the design not only a cordial approval, but with his usual
condescension, promised to write a hymn on the subject proposed to him, ' *The Conversion of England.*'

That noble example of zeal and self denial could not
remain without followers.—Thus the Right Rev. Monsignor
Manning, D.D., Very Rev. Dr. Faber, Very Rev. Canon
Oakeley, Lady Georgiana Fullerton, Rev. H. A. Rawes,
Rev. T. J. Potter, Aubrey de Vere, Esq., and several others
whose names will be seen with pleasure in the following
pages, sent the tribute of their poetical genius to the book of
the Holy Family.

Among the new productions—which amount to one-third
of this collection—some are original compositions, some
translations of foreign or Latin hymns, of which the metre as
well as the idea is preserved,—in many cases a very difficult
task. The rest of the hymns are from the published works
of the above and other poets, who, no less zealous and kind,
opened freely to us their volumes, allowing us to choose and
abridge as suited our purpose.

Thus we have hymns selected from the Oratory Hymn-
book of Dr. Faber, from the Lyra Catholica and other Poems
by Rev. E. Caswall, from the Poems of Aubrey de Vere,
the Hymn-book of the Holy Family at Clapham,* S.
Godrick's Hymn-book, the Catholic Choralist, &c.

This new collection consists of upwards of 100 hymns,
many of which have long been popular in Catholic con-

* All published by Messrs. Burns and Lambert.

gregations, together with such Latin Hymns and Psalms as are most frequently sung in our churches.

It will be seen on perusal that the Holy Family Hymns will be useful to confraternities and congregations generally— a few hymns only having special reference to the Arch-confraternity of the Holy Family. This Hymn-book also will be found valuable as a sacred song book in the workroom or beside the domestic hearth, also for spiritual reading—the order observed in the book giving facility for this.

TUNES.

These Hymns are set to tunes for the most part new in this country; but it is hoped that these tunes having been proved for years and found instruments of great good in Catholic countries, will do their work here as efficiently.

One objection may perhaps strike the *reader* of this music, "*It is so simple: it is so easy.*" It is so, indeed, but this is by design, the hymns being intended for the multitude, for the greatest possible number, for the *people* in fact—and is not the people " almost everybody ?" as some one said.

The tunes chosen are easy, in order to enable the people not only to sing them, but to sing them well, " with grace making melody in their hearts to the Lord !"

These tunes, though simple and easy, are not deficient in real beauty. 'The finest effect I ever heard,' says Haydn, 'did not approach that produced by the uniting of the voices of children in the cathedral; and why,' continues he, ' are not these voices heard in every church and chapel in the land ?'

These tunes are truly beautiful when sung by a large number of men, by a whole congregation. Beautiful also by the *religious expression* which the people will be easily taught to give to their singing. An adequate idea of them can hardly be acquired by merely reading them over, they must be judged of, when used according to their primary design.

The frequent use of *solo* and *chorus* in this Hymn-book calls for remark. The chorus is a sort of abridgment of the whole hymn, a vehement aspiration towards God, a solemn promise or resolution. A few singers best acquainted with the *tune* and words, especially when they are new, sing the stanza or solo, and are replied to with thrilling power by the full chorus of all the voices in the assembly. All can join in the chorus, and the singing receives a new life from it.

The tunes have been revised by the Rev. William Dolan, of Islington, a sufficient guarantee for their correctness.*

Having now completed our explanation, we conclude with a prayer that all who have given us their aid in accomplishing the end designed, and all who shall make use of these Hymns, to aid their devotional feelings, may by the mercy and grace of God, be admitted hereafter to sing together His eternal praises, in the company of the Holy Family, Jesus, Mary, and Joseph.

---

* We have to thank Rev. W. Dolan for the use of his 'Gregorian Hymns,' and the composer of the tunes sung in the Holy Family at Clapham, for some contributions;—also Me. Poussielgue-Rusand de Paris, and Messrs. Burns and Lambert for their generous permission to reprint some music from their hymn-books.

CONTENTS.

—o—

The Nos. to the Hymns and Tunes are the same.
The letters indicate the Hymns now first printed; [O,] original ;
T, translations.

* The Hymns marked with the letters A, B, C, D, &c., have a tune 'noted in the Book of Music.

INDEX OF THE FIRST LINES.

LATIN HYMNS AND TRANSLATIONS.

HOLY FAMILY HYMNS.

I. ALMIGHTY GOD.

1. *The Most Holy Trinity.*

1 Have mercy on us, God Most High!
    Who lift our hearts to Thee;
Have mercy on us, worms of earth,
    Most Holy Trinity!

2 Most ancient of all mysteries!
    Before Thy throne we lie;
Have mercy now, most merciful,
    Most Holy Trinity!

3 When Heaven and earth were yet unmade,
    When time was yet unknown,
Thou in Thy bliss and majesty
    Didst live and love alone!

4 Thou wert not born, there was no fount
    From which Thy Being flowed;
There is no end which Thou canst reach:
    But Thou art simply God.

5 How wonderful creation is!
    The work that Thou didst bless;
And oh! what then must Thou be like,
    Eternal Loveliness!

6 O Majesty most beautiful!
   Most Holy Trinity !
On Mary's throne we climb to get
   A far-off sight of Thee.

7 O listen, then, Most Pitiful!
   To Thy poor creature's heart ;
It blesses Thee that Thou art God,
   That Thou art what Thou art !

8 Most ancient of all mysteries !
   Still at Thy throne we lie ;
Have mercy now, most merciful,
   Most Holy Trinity.

----

2. *The Earth is the Lord's.*

1 Lord of the lords of all the earth !
   Lord of the souls of men !
From Thee all heavenly gifts have birth.
   To Thee return again.

2 The lightnings flashed from off Thy throne,
   Fill heaven and earth with light;
And by that living flame alone,
   Men read the world aright.

3 On every crown and sceptre shed,
   Thy beams of glory shine ;
And burn round every father's head,
   That rules by right divine.

4 The Priests, by Thee anointed, stand,
    Beside his altar, each ;
And all the wise, a prophet-band,
    What Thou hast taught them, teach.

5 And those who heal the sick, and those
    Who plead for the distressed,
Or guard the land from godless foes,
    By Thee are sent, and blessed.

6 Thy voice, O Father, rolls around
    The world for evermore :
The speech we know not, but the sound
    In silence we adore.

7 The heavens themselves repose thereon ;
    Thereon the earth is stayed ;
And seasons change and rivers run,
    By Thee ordained and swayed.

8 The fearful of their cunning boast :
    The haughty of their sword :
But we, and all the heavenly host,
    Will glory in the Lord.

---

3. *Thanksgiving.*

CHORUS.

Benediction and praise,
From our hearts let us raise
To this Lord of grace and love.} Repeat.

1 Praise we our God with joy
    And gladness never ending:
Angels and saints with us
    Their grateful voices blending.
       Chorus.—Benediction, &c.

2 He is our Father dear,
    With Parent's love o'erflowing;
Mercies unsought, unknown,
    On wayward hearts bestowing.
       Chorus.—Benediction, &c.

3 He is our Shepherd true,
    With watchful care unsleeping;
On us, His erring sheep,
    An eye of pity keeping.
       Chorus.—Benediction, &c.

4 He, with a mighty arm,
    The bonds of sin hath broken;
And to our burden'd hearts,
    In words of peace hath spoken.
       Chorus.—Benediction, &c.

5 Bleeding we lay, but He
    With soothing bands hath bound us;
Dark was our path, but He
    Hath poured His light around us.
       Chorus.—Benediction, &c.

6 Graces in copious stream
    From that pure fount are welling,
Where, in our heart of hearts,
    Our God hath set His dwelling.
       Chorus.—Benediction, &c.

7 His word our lantern is,
    His peace our consolation ;
His sweetness all our rest,
    Himself our great salvation.
          Chorus.—Benediction, &c.

8 Then live we all to God,
    On Him in faith relying ;
He be our guide in life,
    Our joy and hope in dying.
          Chorus.—Benediction, &c.

----

4. *Thanksgiving.*

The Music from Beethoven's Choral Symphony,

1 Praise we our God with joy,
    And gladness never ending :
Angels and saints with us
    Their grateful voices blending.

CHORUS.

Thanks and blessing,
Past expressing,
To this tender Lord are due :
Praise we our God with joy,
    And gladness never ending :
Angels and saints with us
    Their grateful voices blending.

2 He is our Father dear,
    With Parent's love o'erflowing ;
Mercies unsought, unknown,
    On wayward hearts bestowing.
          Chorus.—Thanks and blessing, &c.

3 He is our Shepherd true,
  With watchful care unsleeping;
On us, His erring sheep,
  An eye of pity keeping.
        Chorus.—Thanks and blessing, &c.

4 He, with a mighty arm,
  The bonds of sin hath broken,
And to our burden'd hearts,
  In words of peace hath spoken.
        Chorus.—Thanks and blessing, &c.

5 Bleeding we lay, but He
  With soothing bands hath bound us;
Dark was our path, but He
  Hath pour'd His light around us.
        Chorus.—Thanks and blessing, &c.

6 Graces in copious stream
  From that pure fount are welling,
Where, in our heart of hearts,
  Our God hath set His dwelling.
        Chorus.—Thanks and blessing, &c.

7 His word our lantern is,
  His peace our consolation:
His sweetness all our rest,
  Himself our great salvation.
        Chorus.—Thanks and blessing, &c.

8 Then live we all to God,
  On Him in faith relying;
He be our guide in life,
  Our joy and hope in dying.
        Chorus.—Thanks and blessing, &c.

5. *Holy Ghost, come down.*

CHORUS.

Holy Ghost, come down upon Thy children,
  Give us grace, and make us Thine;
Thy tender fires within us kindle,
  Blessed Spirit! Dove Divine!

1 For all within us good and holy
    Is from Thee, Thy precious gift;
  In all our joys, in all our sorrows,
    Wistful hearts to Thee we lift.
        Chorus.—Holy Ghost, come down, &c.

2 For Thou to us art more than father,
    More than sister, in Thy love,
  So gentle, patient and forbearing,
    Holy Spirit! heavenly Dove!
        Chorus.—Holy Ghost, come down, &c.

3 O we have grieved Thee, gracious Spirit,
    Wayward, wanton, cold are we;
  And still our sins, new every morning,
    Never yet have wearied Thee.
        Chorus.—Holy Ghost, come down, &c.

4 Dear Paraclete! how hast Thou waited
    While our hearts were slowly turned,
  How often hath Thy love been slighted
    While for us it grieved and burned.
        Chorus.—Holy Ghost, come down, &c

5 Now if our hearts do not deceive us
  We would take Thee for our Lord;
O dearest Spirit! make us faithful
  To Thy least and lightest word.
      Chorus.—Holy Ghost, come down, &c.

6 Ah! sweet consoler, though we cannot
  Love Thee as Thou lovest us,
Yet if Thou deign'st our hearts to kindle
  They will not be always thus.
      Chorus.—Holy Ghost, come down, &c.

7 With hearts so vile how dare we venture,
  King of Kings, to love Thee so?
And how canst Thou, with such compassion,
  Bear so long with things so low?
      Chorus.— Holy Ghost, come down, &c.

----

6. *Holy Spirit, grant our prayer.*

CHORUS.

Holy Spirit, grant our prayer,
  Inflame our tepid hearts
  With Thy inspiring darts;
Holy Spirit, grant our prayer,
  Inflame our tepid hearts,
  Make Thy dwelling there.

1 Of all gifts Thou giver art,
  In Thy treasures give us part;
  Grant the prayer we pray,
      To Thee this day.
      Chorus.—Holy Spirit, grant, &c.

2 In Thy absence, vainly shine
The stores of gifts divine,
Like a diamond mine ;
Kept from Thee our heart,
    Is sure to smart.
        Chorus.—Holy Spirit, grant, &c.

3 See we wander without sight,
Have compassion on our plight ;
Turn our steps to Thee
        Unceasingly.
        Chorus.—Holy Spirit, grant, &c.

4 On our souls, O God of might,
Send down the joyous light,
Of Thy truth so bright ;
With Thy bounteous hand
        Our hearts expand.
        Chorus.—Holy Spirit, grant, &c.

5 Give to us those pure desires,
Holy tears and purging fires,
Which fill sinners' hearts,
        Touch'd with Thy darts.
        Chorus.—Holy Spirit, grant, &c.

6 Bestow on us docility,
    The gift of purity,
    And of piety,
With a candid mind,
    And spirit kind.
        Chorus.—Holy Spirit, grant, &c.

7 Our tepidity remove,
  Our poor love for Thee improve,
  Give strength to our blows
    Against our foes.
    Chorus.—Holy Spirit, grant, &c.

-----

7.   *Send forth Thy Light, O Lord.*

1 What fire is this within my breast?
  What God, inhabiting my soul?
Thou Giver of the endless rest
  In adoration low I kneel,
Eternal Gladness unexpressed!

CHORUS.

Send forth Thy Light, O Lord,
  And keep us in Thy grace;
Until in heaven we see
  The brightness of Thy Face.

2 The brightness of Thy hidden light
  Is falling on my spirit now,
One glimpse of the entrancing sight,
  In which all saints and angels bow,
Reveals a glory ever-bright.
    Chorus.—Send forth, &c.

3 Dark snares are strewn about my way,
  And enemies are ever round;
Thy light is round me lest I stray,
  Making me walk on sacred ground
And all the night is turned to day.
    Chorus.—Send forth, &c.

4 O God of Light, we turn to Thee,
　　To Thee the Giver of all grace !
Waiting the time when we shall see
　　The unveiled brightness of Thy face,
In depths of Thine eternity.
　　　　Chorus.—Send forth, &c.

5 The splendour of a brighter day
　　·Gleams darkly on our straining eyes ;
Angels of darkness speed away,
　　And from the heaven above the skies
There falls a stronger purer ray.
　　　　Chorus.—Send forth, &c.

6 O God of glory ! Love Divine !
　　Thou Fount of beauty, ever clear,
The white-robed thousands brightly shine
　　Around Thy throne ; and Thou art near
To those who bear a seal of Thine.
　　　　Chorus.—Send forth, &c.

7 Make us Thy temples fair and pure,
　　Blest Paraclete, Eternal Lord !
Thy throne is built for ever sure,
　　One with the Father and the Word !
One God for evermore adored !
　　　　Chorus.—Send forth, &c.

————

8.　*O Holy Ghost, on us descend.*

CHORUS.

O Holy Ghost on us descend,
Thy Spirit with our souls to blend.

Inspire our hearts with burning love, } Repeat.
And to us all Thy goodness prove.

1 Without Thee all is vanity,
   Where Thou art not we wander all astray,
   Oh! dissipate our ignorance we pray,
   Oh! dissipate our ignorance we pray,
   Protect us with Thy ever-watchful eye.
       Chorus.—Oh! Holy Ghost, &c.

2 Hell's demons all endeavour to destroy
   The faithful by this world's seductive snare,
   To undermine our heart's celestial joy,
   Be Thou our heavenly Sov'reign and our Guide,
   All sin to cure, all sorrow to repair.
       Chorus.—Oh! Holy Ghost, &c.

3 Teach us Thy heavenly wisdom, Lord! we pray,
   For that alone our mortal life can bless,
   Along her path the young their mirth display,
   And old age dwells in peaceful happiness.
       Chorus.—Oh! Holy Ghost, &c.

II. OUR BLESSED LORD.

THE SACRED INFANCY.

9. *Christmas Hymn.*

1 The Angels we have heard on high,
   Most sweetly singing o'er our plains,
   And still the mountains in reply
   Are echoing their joyous strains.

CHORUS.

Gloria in excelsis Deo.

2 Say, shepherds, why this Jubilee?
Why thus your rapturous strain prolong?
What may the gladsome tidings be,
Which have inspired your heavenly song?
Chorus.—Gloria, &c.

3 Ah! come to Bethlehem, and see
The Babe whose birth the Angels sing;
Come and adore on bended knee,
The Infant Christ, the new born King.
Chorus.—Gloria, &c.

4 See Jesus in a manger laid,
'Tis He whom choirs of Angels praise,
Mary and Joseph lend your aid,
Our hearts in love to Jesus raise.
Chorus.—Gloria, &c.

___

10. *The Infant Saviour.*

1 See, amid the winter's snow,
Born for us on earth below,
See, the tender Lamb appears,
Promis'd from eternal years!

CHORUS.

Hail, thou ever blessed morn!
Hail, Redemption's happy dawn!
Sing through all Jerusalem,
Christ is born in Bethlehem.

2 Lo, within a manger lies
  He who built the starry skies;
  He, who thron'd in height sublime
  Sits amid the Cherubim!
    Chorus.—Hail, &c.

3 Say, ye holy shepherds, say,
  What your joyful news to-day;
  Wherefore have ye left your sheep
  On the lonely mountain steep?
    Chorus.—Hail, &c.

4 "As we watched at dead of night,
  Lo, we saw a wondrous light;
  Angels singing peace on earth,
  Told us of the Saviour's birth."
    Chorus.—Hail, &c.

5 Sacred infant all divine,
  What a tender love was Thine;
  Thus to come from highest bliss,
  Down to such a world as this!
    Chorus.—Hail, &c.

6 Teach, O teach us, holy Child,
  By Thy face so meek and mild,
  Teach us to resemble Thee,
  In Thy sweet humility!
    Chorus.—Hail, &c.

7 Virgin Mother, Mary blest,
  By the joys that fill thy breast,
  Pray for us that we may prove
  Worthy of our Saviour's love.
    Chorus.—Hail, &c.

11. *Jesus and Mary.*

1 Oft as Thee, my infant Saviour,
   In Thy mother's arms I view,
Straight a thousand thrilling raptures
   Overflow my heart anew.

CHORUS.

Happy Babe! and happy Mother!
   O how great your bliss must be!
Each enfolded in the other,
   Sipping pure felicity!

2 As the sun from darkness springing
   Breathes a charm o'er nature's face;
So the Child to Mary clinging,
   Decks her with diviner grace.
        Chorus.—Happy Babe! &c.

3 As the limpid dew descending
   Lies impearl'd upon the rose;
So their mutual beauty blending
   In transporting union glows.
        Chorus.—Happy Babe! &c.

4 As when early spring advances,
   Flowers unnumbered throng the mead;
Such the countless loving glances
   That in turn from each proceed.
        Chorus.—Happy Babe! &c.

5 Lovely Jesu! gentle Brother!
   How I wish a smile from Thee,
Meant for Thy immortal Mother,
   Only might alight on me!
        Chorus.—Happy Babe! &c.

12. *Dear Little One.*

Repeat the last line of every verse.

1 Dear Little One! how sweet Thou art,
    Thine eyes how bright they shine,
So bright they almost seem to speak
    When Mary's look meets Thine!

How faint and feeble is Thy cry,
    Like plaint of harmless dove,
When Thou dost murmur in Thy sleep
    Of sorrow and of love!

2 When Mary bids Thee sleep, Thou sleep'st,
    Thou wakest when she calls;
Thou art content upon her lap,
    Or in the rugged stalls.

Simplest of Babes! with what a grace
    Thou dost Thy Mother's will!
Thine infant fashions well betray
    The Godhead's hidden skill.

3 When Joseph takes Thee in his arms,
    And smooths Thy little cheek,
Thou lookest up into his face
    So helpless and so meek.

Yes! Thou art what Thou seem'st to be,
    A thing of smiles and tears;
Yet Thou art God, and heaven and earth
    Adore Thee with their fears.

4 Yes! dearest Babe! those tiny hands,
  That play with Mary's hair,
The weight of all the mighty world
  This very moment bear.
    Art Thou, weak Babe, my very God?
    O I must love Thee then,
Love Thee, and yearn to spread Thy love
  Among forgetful men.

---

13.   *The Infant Jesus asleep.*

1   Sleep, holy Babe,
  Upon Thy mother's breast;
Great Lord of earth and sea and sky,
How sweet it is to see Thee lie
    In such a place of rest!
    Sleep, holy Babe! Sleep, holy Babe!

2   Sleep, holy Babe!
  Thine angels watch around;
All bending low, with folded wings,
Before th' Incarnate King of kings.
    In reverent awe profound.
    Sleep, holy Babe! Sleep, holy Babe!

3   Sleep, holy Babe!
  While I with Mary gaze
In joy upon that face awhile,
Upon the loving infant smile,
    Which there divinely plays.
    Sleep, holy Babe! Sleep, holy Babe!

4   Sleep, holy Babe!
Ah, take Thy brief repose ;
Too quickly will Thy slumbers break,
And Thou to lengthen'd pains awake,
    That death alone shall close.
    Sleep, holy Babe ! Sleep, holy Babe !

5   Then must those hands,
    Which now so fair I see ;
Those little pearly feet of Thine,
So soft, so delicately fine,
    Be pierc'd and rent for me !
    O cruel wounds ! O cruel wounds !

6   Then must that brow
    Its thorny crown receive ;
That cheek, more lovely than the rose,
Be drench'd with blood, and marr'd with blows,
    That I thereby may live.
    O cruel sin ! O cruel sin !

7   O Lady blest !
Sweet Virgin, hear my cry !
Forgive the wrong that I have done,
To thee, in causing thy dear Son,
    Upon the cross to die !
    O Lady blest ! O Lady blest !

————

14.   *The Infant Jesus in the crib.*
(From St. Alphonso.)

1 O King of Heaven ! from starry throne de-
    scending,
    Thou takest refuge in that wretched cave ;

O God of bliss! I see Thee cold and trembling,
What pain it cost Thee, fallen man to save!

CHORUS.

Sweet Infant Jesus!
Infant divine!
Make me, oh make me,
For ever be Thine!

2 Thou, of a thousand worlds the great Creator,
Dost now the pain of cold and want endure;
Thy poverty but makes Thee more endearing,
For well I know, 'tis love has made Thee
poor.
Chorus.—Sweet Infant Jesus, &c.

3 I see Thee leave Thy heavenly Father's bosom—
But whither has Thy love transported Thee?
Upon a little straw I see Thee lying:
Why suffer Thus? 'Tis all for love of me.
Chorus.—Sweet Infant Jesus, &c.

4 But if it is Thy Will for me to suffer,
And by these sufferings my heart to move;
Wherefore, my Jesus, do I see Thee weeping?
'Tis not for pain Thou weepest, but for love.
Chorus.—Sweet Infant Jesus, &c.

5 Thou weepest thus, to see me so ungrateful;
My sins have pierced Thee to the very core;
I once despised Thy love,—but now I love Thee,
I love but Thee,—then, Jesus weep no more.
Chorus.—Sweet Infant Jesus, &c.

6 Thou sleepest, Lord, but Thy heart ever
　　watches,
　　No slumber can a heart so loving take ;
　But tell me, darling Babe, of what Thou
　　thinkest—
　　　" I think," He says, " of dying for thy sake."
　　　Chorus.—Sweet Infant Jesus, &c.

7 Is it for me, that Thou dost think of dying ?
　　What then, O Jesus, can I love but Thee !
　Mary, my hope ! if I love Him too little,
　　Be not indignant—love Him thou for me,
　　　Chorus.—Sweet Infant Jesus, &c.

15.　*The Epiphany.*

(Repeat the two last lines of every verse.)

1 They leave the land of gems and gold,
　　The shining portals of the East ;
　For Him, " the Woman's Seed " foretold,
　　They leave the revel, and the feast.

2 To earth their sceptres they have cast,
　　And crowns by kings ancestral worn ;
　They track the lonely Syrian waste ;
　　They kneel before the Babe new-born.

3 O happy eyes, that saw Him first !
　　O happy lips that kissed His feet !
　Earth slakes at last her ancient thirst :
　　With Eden's joy her pulses beat.

4 True kings are those who thus forsake
　　Their kingdoms for the Eternal King—

Serpent! Her foot is on thy neck!
Herod! thou writh'st, but canst not sting!

5 He, He is King, and He alone,
Who lifts that infant hand to bless;
Who makes His mother's knee His throne,
Yet rules the starry wilderness.

THE PASSION.

16. *Hail Wounds.*

1 Hail wounds! which through eternal years
The love of Jesus shew;
Hail wounds! from whence encrimson'd rills
Of blood for ever flow.

More precious than the gems of Ind,
Than all the stars more fair;
Nor honeycomb, nor fragrant rose,
Can once with you compare.

2 Through you is open'd to our souls
A refuge safe and calm,
Whither no raging enemy
Can reach to work us harm.

What countless stripes did Christ receive
Naked in Pilate's hall!
From His torn flesh what streams of blood
Did all around Him fall!

3 How doth th' ensanguin'd thorny crown
That beauteous brow transpierce!
How do the nails those hands and feet
Contract with tortures fierce!

He bows His head, and forth at last
　　His loving spirit soars ;
Yet even after death His heart
　　For us its tribute pours.

4 Beneath the wine-press of God's wrath
　　His Blood for us He drains ;
Till for Himself, O wondrous love !
　　No single drop remains.

Oh, come all ye in whom are fix'd
　　The deadly stains of sin !
Come ! wash in this all-saving Blood,
　　And ye shall be made clean.

————

17. *'O'erwhelm'd in depths of woe.'*

1 O'erwhelm'd in depths of woe,
　　Upon the tree of scorn
Hangs the Redeemer of mankind,
　　With racking anguish torn.

2 See ! how the nails those hands
　　And feet so tender rend ;
See ! down His face, and neck, and breast,
　　His sacred Blood descend.

3 Hark ! with what awful cry
　　His spirit takes its flight ;
That cry, it pierced the Mother's heart,
　　And whelm'd her soul in night.

4 Earth hears, and to its base
　　Rocks wildly to and fro ;

Tombs burst; seas, rivers, mountains quake;
  The veil is rent in two.

5 The sun withdraws his light;
  The midday heav'ns grow pale;
The moon, and stars, the universe,
  Their Maker's death bewail.

6 Shall man alone be mute?
  Come, youth! and hoary hairs!
Come, rich and poor! come, all mankind!
  And bathe those feet in tears.

7 Come! fall before His Cross,
  Who shed for us His blood:
Who died the Victim of pure love,
  To make us sons of God.

8 Jesu! all praise to Thee,
  Our joy and endless rest!
Be Thou our guide while pilgrims here,
  Our crown amid the blest.

18. *The Passion of Jesus.*
(From St. Alphonso.)

1 My Jesus! say, what wretch has dared
  Thy sacred hands to bind?
And who has dared to buffet so
  Thy face so meek and kind?

CHORUS.
'Tis I have thus ungrateful been,
  Yet, Jesus! pity take!
Oh spare and pardon me, my Lord,
  For Thy sweet mercy's sake!

2 My Jesus! who with spittle vile
    Profaned Thy sacred brow?
Or whose unpitying scourge has made
    Thy precious blood to flow?
          Chorus.—'Tis I have thus, &c.

3 My Jesus! whose the hands that wove
    That cruel thorny crown?
Who made that hard and heavy cross
    That weighs Thy shoulders down?
          Chorus.—'Tis I have thus, &c.

4 My Jesus! who has mocked Thy thirst
    With vinegar and gall;
Who held the nails that pierced Thy hands,
    And made the hammer fall?
          Chorus.—'Tis I have thus, &c.

5 My Jesus! say, who dared to nail
    Those tender feet of Thine;
And whose the arm that raised the lance
    To pierce that Heart divine?
          Chorus.—'Tis I have thus, &c.

6 And, Mary! who has murdered thus,
    Thy lov'd and only One?
Canst thou forgive the blood-stained hand
    That robbed thee of thy Son?

CHORUS.

'Tis I have thus ungrateful been
    To Jesus and to thee;
Forgive me for thy Jesus' sake,
    And pray to Him for me.

19. *Jesus Crucified.*

1 O come and mourn with me awhile;
See, Mary calls us to her side;
O come and let us mourn with her:
Jesus, our Love, is crucified!

2 Have we no tears to shed for Him,
While soldiers scoff and Jews deride?
Ah, look how patiently He hangs:
Jesus, our Love, is crucified!

3 How fast His hands and feet are nailed;
His Blessed Tongue with thirst is tied:
His failing Eyes are blind with blood:
Jesus, our Love, is crucified!

4 His Mother cannot reach His face!
She stands in helplessness beside;
Her heart is martyred with her Son's:
Jesus, our Love, is crucified!

5 Seven times He spoke, seven words of love,
And all three hours His silence cried
For mercy on the souls of men:
Jesus, our Love, is crucified!

6 What was Thy crime, my dearest Lord?
By earth, by heaven, Thou hast been tried,
And guilty found of too much love:
Jesus, our Love, is crucified! ..

THE RESURRECTION.

20. *Jesus Risen.*

Repeat the last two lines of every verse.

1 All hail! dear Conqueror! All hail!
  O what a victory is Thine!
  How beautiful Thy strength appears,
  Thy crimson wounds how bright they shine!

2 Thou camest at the dawn of day;
  Armies of souls around Thee were,
  Blessed spirits thronging to adore
  Thy Flesh, so marvellous, so fair.

3 The everlasting Godhead lay
  Shrouded within those Limbs Divine,
  Nor left untenanted one hour
  That Sacred Human Heart of Thine.

4 They worshipped Thee, those ransomed souls,
  With the fresh strength of love let free;
  They worshipped joyously, and thought
  Of Mary while they looked on Thee.

5 And Thou too, Soul of Jesus, Thou
  Towards that sacred Flesh didst yearn,
  And for the beatings of that Heart
  How ardently Thy love did burn!

6 They worshipped while the beauteous Soul
  Paused by the Body's wounded side:—
  Bright flashed the cave—before them stood
  The Living Jesus Glorified.

7 Down, down, all lofty things on earth,
　And worship Him with joyous dread!
　O Sin! thou art undone by love!
　O Death! thou art discomfited!

8 Ye Heavens, how sang they in your courts,
　How sang the angelic choirs that day,
　When from His tomb, the imprisoned God,
　Like the strong sunrise, broke away!

9 O I am burning so with love,
　I fear lest I should make too free;
　Let me lie silent and adore
　Thy glorified Humanity.

10 Ah! now Thou sendest me sweet tears;
　Fluttered with love, my spirits fail,—
　What shall I say? Thou know'st my heart;
　All hail! dear Conqueror! all hail.

THE BLESSED SACRAMENT.

21. *Sweet Sacrament.*

1 Jesus! my Lord, my God, my all!
　How can I love Thee as I ought?
And how revere this wondrous gift,
　So far surpassing hope or thought?

CHORUS.

Sweet Sacrament! we Thee adore!
Oh, make us love Thee more and more!

2 Had I but Mary's sinless heart
　To love Thee with, my dearest King,

Oh, with what bursts of fervent praise
Thy goodness, Jesus, would I sing !
           Chorus.—Sweet Sacrament, &c.

3 O see ! within a creature's hand
   The vast Creator deigns to be,
Reposing infant-like, as though
   On Joseph's arm, or Mary's knee.
           Chorus.—Sweet Sacrament, &c.

4 Thy Body, Soul, and Godhead, all !
   O mystery of love divine !
I cannot compass all I have ;
   For all Thou hast and art are mine !
           Chorus.—Sweet Sacrament, &c.

5 Sound, sound His praises higher still,
   And come, ye angels, to our aid ;
'Tis God ! 'tis God ! the very God
   Whose power both man and angels made !
           Chorus.—Sweet Sacrament, &c.

6 He comes ! He comes ! the Lord of Hosts,
   Borne on His throne triumphantly !
We see Thee, and we know Thee, Lord ;
   And yearn to shed our blood for Thee.
           Chorus.—Sweet Sacrament, &c.

7 Our hearts leap up ; our trembling song
   Grows fainter still ; we can no more ;
Silence ! and let us weep—and die
   Of very love, while we adore.

CHORUS.

Great Sacrament of love divine !
All, all we have or are be Thine.

22. *The Elevation of the Host.*

1 In breathless silence kneel,
With trembling rapture feel
The hour of grace is nigh;
Watch for the signal given,
As for a voice from heaven,
The Lord is standing by.

CHORUS.

Hush! Hush! Break not the spell!
Jesus is here; our hearts know it well.
Kneel! Kneel! in love and fear;
Jesus is God and Jesus is here.
Hark to the sound of the Sanctuary bell,
(One voice.) *(All.)*
Telling of love, burning for ever, ⎱ Repeat.
(One voice.) *(All.)* ⎰
For ever, for ever!

2 Stir not the silent air,
E'en by the words of prayer,
Breathe not too loud a sigh,
In your heart's deep recess,
Your fears, your hopes express,
Send up a speechless cry.
    Chorus.—Hush! Hush! &c.

3 Mute be the organ's strain,
Man's voice of praise is vain,
When God is all in all.
Speak not, let words alone;
Be still, His presence own,
Before Him prostrate fall.
    Chorus.—Hush! Hush! &c.

4 This is no common hour,
  This is no human power,
  God is among you now ;
  And each full heart may share
  In Peter's raptured prayer
  On the lone mountain's brow.
          Chorus.—Hush ! Hush ! &c,

---

23. *'O what Wonders of Love,'*

1 O what wonders of love, on the altar I see,
  From the Host, our dear Lord is looking on me ;
  He looks on the creature, He died to redeem ;
  How great is His love, how small must mine
      seem !

CHORUS.

  O dearest Lord ! teach me to love }
  As do the saints in heaven above. } Repeat.

2 O my Jesus how long on the earth must I stay
  Before to Thy Bosom, my soul flies away ?
  My exile then over, I trust by Thy grace
  To enter Thy presence, and see Thy sweet Face.

CHORUS.

  O dearest Lord ! I burn with love, }
  Oh take me home, to Thee above. } Repeat

24 *' My God, my Life, my Love.'*

CHORUS.

My God, my life, my love!
  To Thee, to Thee, I call!
O come to me from heav'n above,
  And be my God, my all!

1 My faith beholds Thee, Lord,
    Conceal'd in human food;
  My senses fail; but on Thy word,
    I trust and find my God.
      Chorus.—My God, &c.

2 O when wilt Thou be mine!
    Sweet lover of my soul,
  My Jesus dear, my King divine,—
    And all my heart control!
      Chorus.—My God, &c.

3 O come and fix Thy throne
    Within my very heart;
  O make it burn for Thee alone,
    For Thou its master art.
      Chorus.—My God, &c.

4 On Thee I stay my mind,
    For vain are earthly toys;
  In Thee alone my life I find
    The joy of heaven's joys!
      Chorus.—My God, &c.

25. *Bread of Life.*

1 When by Thy altar, Lord, I kneel,
  And think upon Thy love ;
  O make my heart Thy goodness feel,
  Fix it on things above !

CHORUS.

  My sweetest Lord, when I retrace
  Thy wondrous love for me ;
  Oh! how can I affection place
  On anything but Thee?

2 About to leave this wretched earth,
  On man Thy thoughts still bent,
  Thy sacred, boundless love, gave birth,
  To this sweet Sacrament :
  Chorus.—My sweetest Lord, &c.

3 Oh manna! which my Sov'reign Lord
  In pity left for me ;
  Without this mystery adored
  What would this exile be?
  Chorus.—My sweetest Lord, &c.

4 A desert land of woe and care,
  A pilgrimage of strife,
  Who could its grief, its sorrows bear,
  Without this Bread of Life ?
  Chorus.—My sweetest Lord, &c.

5 My soul here finds a sov'reign balm,
  A cure for every grief,
  'Mid pain and care a heavenly calm,
  A solace and relief.
  Chorus.—My sweetest Lord, &c.

6 Supported by this Heavenly Bread,
   My Lord's last pledge of love ;
With joy the rugged path I'll tread,
   To Horeb's mount above.
      Chorus.—My sweetest Lord, &c.

7 Strengthened by this, my soul its flight,
   Shall from this exile soar,
To dwell in realms of bliss and light
   For ever, evermore.
      Chorus.—My sweetest Lord, &c.

-----

26. *The Altar.*

1 O happy Flowers! O happy Flowers!
How quietly for hours and hours,
In dead of night, in cheerful day,
Close to my own dear Lord you stay,
Until you gently fade away!
O happy Flowers! what would I give,
In your sweet place all day to live,
And then to die, my service o'er,
Softly as you do, at His door.

2 O happy Lights! O happy Lights!
Watching my Jesus livelong nights,
How close you cluster round His throne,
Dying so meekly one by one,
As each its faithful watch has done.
Could I with you but take my turn,
And burn with love of Him, and burn
Till love had wasted me, like you,
Sweet Lights! what better could I do?

3 O happy Pyx! O happy Pyx!
Where Jesus doth His dwelling fix;
O little palace, dear and bright,
Where He, Who is the world's true light,
Spends all the day, and stays all night—
Ah! if my heart could only be
A little home for Him like thee,
Such fires my happy soul would move,
I could not help but die of love!

4 O Pyx and Lights and Flowers! but I
Through envy of you will not die;
Nay, happy things! what will you do,
For I am better off than you,
The whole day long, the whole night through:
For Jesus gives Himself to me
So sweetly and so utterly:
By rights, long since I should have died,
For love of Jesus crucified.

5 My happy Soul! My happy Soul!
How shall I then my love control?
O sweet Communion! Feast of bliss!
When the dear Host my tongue doth kiss,
What happiness is like to this?
O heaven, I think, must be alway
Quite like a First Communion day;
With love so sweet and joy so strange,—
Only that heaven will never change!

27. *Thanksgiving after Communion.*

1 What happiness can equal mine ?
   I've found the object of my love ;
My Saviour and my Lord divine
   Is come to me from heaven above.
He makes my heart His own abode,
   His flesh becomes my daily bread ;
He pours on me His healing blood,
   And with His life my soul is fed.

2 My Love is mine, and I am His ;
   In me He dwells, in Him I live :
Where could I taste a purer bliss?
   What greater boon could Jesus give?
O royal banquet ! heavenly feast !
   O flowing fount of life and grace !
Where God the Giver, man the guest,
   Meet and unite in sweet embrace.

3 Dear Jesus, now my heart is Thine,
   Oh ! may it never from Thee fly ;
My God, be Thou for ever mine,
   And I Thine own eternally.
No more, O Satan, thee I fear !
   O world ! thy charms I now despise !
For Christ Himself is with me here,
   My joy, my life, my paradise.

28. *Visit to the Blessed Sacrament.*

Repeat the last line of every verse.

1 Before the altar angels veil their faces,
   For God is dwelling there by night and day:
His Heart is full of love, His Hands of graces,
   With which He crowns the souls that come
      to pray.
      To His presence returning,
      With our hearts brightly burning,
We come to kneel before His sacred feet,
To see His face and hear His words so sweet.

2 Oh sinner come! fear not a wrathful sentence,
   For blessed are the tears which sinners weep;
The angels all rejoice at man's repentance,
   And Jesus came to save the wandering sheep.
      He receives the offender
      With compassion so tender
That tears of sorrow turn to tears of joy,
Which wash out sin and earthly love destroy.

3 To Jesus come, all you who weak and weary
   Begin to faint beneath your heavy load,
And He will cheer your spirits sad and dreary,
   He bears His cross before you on the road;
      His example will move us
      And His patience reprove us,
Encouraged thus we'll gladly bear our pain,
To show our love, and heavenly bliss to gain.

4 Oh dearest Lord Thy Sacred Heart is yearn-
  ing,
    To gather souls around Thy humble throne,
Increase the flame with which our love is
    burning,
    Oh take our hearts and make them like Thine
    Own.
      Thy sweet blessing bespeaking,
      We, Thy children, are seeking,
The crowning grace to love Thee here below,
And after death to Thee above to go.

THE SACRED HEART.

29. *O Sacred Heart!*

1 O Sacred Heart!
Our home lies deep in Thee.
On earth Thou art an exile's rest,
In heaven the glory of the blest,
    O Sacred Heart.

2 O Sacred Heart,
  Thou fount of contrite tears,
Where'er those living waters flow,
New life to sinners they bestow,
    O Sacred Heart.

3 O Sacred Heart,
  Bless our dear Fatherland,
May Erin's sons to truth e'er stand,
With faith's bright banner still in hand.
    O Sacred Heart.

4   O Sacred Heart,
   Watch o'er our sister isle,
Till faith ere long, return once more
And find a home on England's shore.
      O Sacred Heart!

5   O Sacred Heart,
   Our trust is all in Thee ;
For though earth's night be dark and dreai,
Thou breathest rest, where Thou art near,
      O Sacred Heart.

6   O Sacred Heart,
   When shades of death shall fall,
Receive us 'neath Thy gentle care,
And save us from the tempter's snare :
      O Sacred Heart.

7   O Sacred Heart,
   Lead exiled children home,
Where we may ever rest near Thee,
In peace and joy eternally,
      O Sacred Heart.

---

30.   *To Christ, the Prince of Peace.*

CHORUS.

To Christ, the Prince of Peace,
   And Son of God most High,
The Father of the world to come,
   Sing we with holy joy.

1 Deep in His Heart for us
   The wound of love He bore ;
That love with which He still inflames
   The hearts that Him adore.

2 O Jesu ! Victim blest !
   What else but love divine
Could Thee constrain to open thus
   That Sacred Heart of Thine ?

3 O fount of endless life !
   O spring of waters clear !
O flame celestial, cleansing all
   Who unto Thee draw near.

4 Hide me in Thy dear Heart ;
   For thither do I fly ;
There seek Thy grace through life, in death
   Thine immortality.

5 Praise to the Father be ;
   Praise to His only Son ;
Praise to the blessed Paraclete,
   While endless ages run.

---

31. *The True Shepherd.*

1 I was wandering and weary,
   When my Saviour came unto me ;
For the ways of sin grew dreary,
   And the world had ceased to woo me :

And I thought I heard Him say,
As He came along His way,
  O silly souls! come near me,
  My sheep should never fear me;
    I am, I am the Shepherd true.

2 At first I would not hearken,
  And put off till the morrow;
But life began to darken,
  And I was sick with sorrow;
And I thought, &c. (as in verse 1.)

3 At last I stopped to listen,
  His voice could not deceive me;
I saw His kind eyes glisten,
  So anxious to relieve me:
And I thought, &c. (as in verse 1.)

4 He took me on His shoulder,
  And tenderly He kissed me;
He bade my love be bolder,
  And said how He had missed me;
And I'm sure I heard Him say,
As He went along His way, &c. (as in v. 1.)

5 Strange gladness seemed to move Him,
  Whenever I did better;
And He coaxed me so to love Him,
  As if He was my debtor:
And I always heard Him say,
As He went along His way, &c. (as in v. 1.)

6 I thought His love would weaken,
  As more and more He knew me:
But it burneth like a beacon,
  And its light and heat go through me;

And I ever hear Him say,
As He goes along His way, &c. (as in v. 1.)

7 Let us do then, dearest brothers,
    What will best and longest please us ;
Follow not the ways of others,
    But trust ourselves to Jesus:
We shall ever hear Him say,
As He goes along His way,
    O silly souls come near Me ;
    My sheep should never fear me ;
    I am, I am the Shepherd true.

---

32. *Jesus, the very thought of Thee.*

CHORUS.

Jesus ! the very thought of Thee
    With sweetness fills my breast,
But sweeter far Thy face to see,
    And in Thy presence rest.

1 Nor voice can sing, nor heart can frame,
    Nor can the memory find,
A sweeter sound than Thy blest Name,
    O Saviour of mankind !
        Chorus.—Jesus, &c.

2 O hope of every contrite heart,
    O joy of all the meek,
To those who fall, how kind Thou art:
    How good to those who seek !
        Chorus.—Jesus, &c.

3 But what to those who find?　Ah ! this
　　Nor tongue, nor pen can shew ;
　The love of Jesus, what it is,
　　None but His lov'd ones know.
　　　　Chorus.—Jesus, &c.

4 Jesus, our only joy be Thou,
　　As Thou our prize wilt be ;
　Jesus, be Thou our glory now,
　　Our hope, our victory.　　　　　·
　　　　Chorus.—Jesus, &c.

5 O Jesu ! spotless virgin flower !
　　Our life and joy ! to Thee
　Be praise, beatitude and power,
　　Through all eternity.
　　　　Chorus.—Jesus, &c.

————

33.　*Evening Hymn to Jesus.*

1 Hear Thy children, gentle Jesus,
　　While we breathe our evening prayer,
　Save us from all harm and danger,
　　Take us 'neath Thy shelt'ring care.

2 Save us from the wiles of Satan,
　　'Mid the lone and sleepful night,
　Sweetly may bright guardian angels
　　Keep us 'neath their watchful sight.

3 Gentle Jesus, look in pity
　　From Thy great white throne above,
　All the night Thy Heart is wakeful
　　In Thy sacrament of love.

4 Shades of even fast are falling,
    Day is fading into gloom,
When the shades of death fall round us,
    Lead Thine exiled children home.

III. THE BLESSED VIRGIN MARY.

34. *St. Casimir's Hymn.*

Translated and selected by H. E. C. W.

1   Sing, sing, each day,
      A tuneful lay,
  My soul, to Mary's glory:
      Her feasts employ
      With pious joy
  To con her wondrous story.

2   Unending lays
      Sound forth her praise,
  The Queen of all created:
      Till note on note
      Through Heaven float,
  Each with her goodness freighted.

3   A sentence dire,
      From God's just ire,
  Bore man for Eve's transgression;
      Till Mary led
      The spendthrift's tread
  Back home from sin's oppression.

4   O blessed shoot
From Jesse's root
Hope, refuge of minds weary !
The earth's delight,
The abyss's light,
The Lord's own sanctuary.

5   Most precious gem !
Rose-budding stem !
O lily of pure saintliness !
Chaste virgin-trains
To blissful reigns
Lead up thy queenly stateliness.

6   Virgin rejoice,
Whom every voice,
Should join in glorifying ;
Whose first sweet look
The prison shook,
Where hopeless man lay sighing.

7   The Virgin's flower,
The Mother's dower,
Thy gifts are to eternity ;
The palm tree shedding
Its fruits, yet budding,
Is type of thy maternity.

8   For when thy birth
Gave joy, the earth
With radiant vest adorning,
It cast away
The dark array
Of ages spent in mourning.

9 For this I cry,
  For this I sigh,
 Be thou my soul's physician !
  Thy gifts of grace,
  Poured down apace,
 Requite my soul's petition.

10 Cherish, sustain,
  The suppliant train
 In thy sweet prayer confiding !
  Whatever pains,
  Whatever stains
 Prevent in us abiding.

35. *The Immaculate Conception.*

1 " And can it be, that God should deign
 " Like men to be of sinners born,
 " From those on whom His curse hath lain,
 " The creatures of a world forlorn ?

CHORUS.

" Our God is great, our God is high,—yes high !
 " His praise is heard above the sky !
" Nor may there aught of sin draw nigh,—not
 nigh !
 " To where His sov'reign might—
 " —— His sov'reign might doth lie."

2 Thus spoke the gazing cherubim,
  When first they heard the law of love ;
 When first they saw in vision dim,
  The work of the descending Dove.

3 Yet lovingly they paused, amaz'd,
    And own'd themselves as creatures frail,
The wisdom of their God they prais'd,
    Whose love, whose bounty could not fail.
        Chorus.—Our God is great, &c.

4 Then to the heavenly host there came
    A message of peculiar grace:
" A woman without sin proclaim
    "Sole parent of a heavenly race."
        Chorus.—Our God is great, &c.

5 The joyful sound is heard on high,
    For She whose being now is sung,
To God Himself is very nigh,
    As Mother, prais'd by every tongue.
        Chorus.—Our God is great, &c.

6 The Word eternal,—Heav'n's great Lord,
    Will own her by that title blest,
And Heav'n's glad hosts in sweet accord
    Will learn submissive her behest.
        Chorus.—Our God is great, &c.

7 Yes, Virgin Queen, Immaculate,
    Our tongues, our thoughts, are all too frail
To tell the greatness of thy state,
    And all thy glory to detail.
        Chorus.—Our God is great, &c.

8 Yet fearlessly we may thee bless,
    For childhood's weakness thou canst own,
Since, Pure One! 'twas by lowliness
    Thou cam'st to God's eternal throne.
        Chorus.—Our God is great, &c.

36.   *'O purest of Creatures!'*

1 O purest of creatures! sweet Mother! sweet
    Maid!
The one spotless womb wherein Jesus was laid!
Dark night hath come down on us, Mother!
    and we,
Look out for thy shining, sweet Star of the Sea!

2 Deep night hath come down on this rough-
    spoken world,
And the banners of darkness are boldly unfurled;
And the tempest-tossed Church—all her eyes
    are on thee,
They look to thy shining, sweet Star of the Sea!

3 The Church doth what God had first taught
    her to do;
He looked o'er the world, to find hearts that
    were true;
Through the ages He looked, and He found
    none but thee,
And He loved thy clear shining, sweet Star of
    the Sea!

4 He gazed on thy soul; it was spotless and fair;
  For the empire of sin—it had never been there;
  None had e'er owned thee, dear Mother! but
    He,
  And He blessed thy clear shining, sweet Star
    of the Sea!

5 Earth gave Him one lodging; 'twas deep in
    thy breast,
  And God found a home, where the sinner finds
    rest,
  His home and His hiding-place, both were in
    thee,
  He was won by thy shining, sweet Star of the
    Sea!

6 O blissful and calm was the wonderful rest
  That thou gavest thy God in thy virginal breast;
  For the heaven He left He found heaven in
    thee,
  And He shone in thy shining, sweet Star of
    the Sea!

---

37. *Immaculate! Immaculate!*

1 O mother! I could weep for mirth,
    Joy fills my heart so fast;
  My soul to-day is heaven on earth,
    O could the transport last!

CHORUS.

I think of thee, and what thou art,
Thy majesty, thy state ;
And I keep singing in my heart—
Immaculate! Immaculate.

2 When Jesus looks upon thy face,
His heart with rapture glows,
And in the church, by His sweet grace,
Thy blessed worship grows.
Chorus.—I think of thee, &c.

3 The Angels answer with their songs,
Bright choirs in gleaming rows ;
And saints flock round thy feet in throngs,
And Heaven with bliss o'erflows.
Chorus.—I think of thee, &c.

4 Conceived, conceived Immaculate !
O what a joy for thee !
Conceived, conceived Immaculate !
O greater joy for me !
Chorus.—I think of thee, &c.

5 It is this thought to-day that lifts
My happy heart to heaven,
That for our sakes thy choicest gifts
To thee, dear Queen ! were given.
Chorus.—I think of thee, &c.

6 O blessed be the Eternal Son
Who joys to call thee mother ;
And lets poor men, by sin undone,
For thy sake call Him brother.
Chorus.—I think of thee, &c.

38. *The Nativity of the Blessed Virgin.*

1 Sweet Morn! thou parent of the sun!
  And daughter of the same!
What joy and gladness, through thy birth,
  This day to mortals came!

Cloth'd in the sun, I see thee stand,
  The moon beneath thy feet;
The stars above thy sacred head
  A radiant coronet.
    Repeat.—Sweet Morn, &c.

2 Thrones and dominions gird thee round,
  The armies of the sky,
Pure streams of glory from thee flow
  All bath'd in Deity!

Terrific as the banner'd line
  Of battle's dread array,
Before thee tremble hell and death,
  And own thy potent sway:
    Repeat.—Sweet Morn, &c.

3 While crush'd beneath thy dauntless foot,
  The serpent writhes in vain;
Smote by a deadly stroke, and bound
  In an eternal chain.

O Mightiest! pray for us, that He
  Who came through thee of yore,
May come to dwell within our hearts,
  And never quit us more.
    Repeat.—Sweet Morn, &c.

39. *Our Lady's Expectation.*

1 Like the dawning of the morning,
    On the mountain's golden heights,
Like the breaking of the moonbeams
    On the gloom of cloudy nights,
Like a secret told by angels,
    Getting known upon the earth,
Is the Mother's Expectation
    Of Messiah's speedy birth!

2 Thou wert happy, blessed Mother!
    With the very bliss of heaven,
Since the angel's salutation
    In thy raptured ear was given;
Since the Ave of that midnight,
    When thou wert anointed Queen,
Like a river overflowing
    Hath the grace within thee been.

3 O the feeling of thy Burden,
    It was touch, and taste, and sight:
It was newer still and newer,
    All those nine months, day and night
Like a treasure unexhausted,
    Like a vision unconfess'd,
Like a rapture unforgotten
    It lay ever at thy breast.

4 Every moment did that Burden,
    Press upon thee with new grace;
Happy Mother! thou art longing
    To behold the Saviour's Face!

O, His human face and features
Must be passing sweet to see;
Thou hast seen them, happy Mother!
O then, show them now to me.

---

40. *The Sorrows of the B. V. M.*

Repeat the two last lines of each verse.

1 What a sea of tears and sorrow
Did the soul of Mary toss
To and fro upon its billows,
While she wept her bitter loss;
In her arms her Jesus holding,
Torn.but newly from the cross!

2 O that mournful Virgin Mother!
See her tears how fast they flow
Down upon His mangled body,
Wounded side, and thorny brow;
While His hands and feet she kisses,—
Picture of immortal woe!

3 Oft and oft His arms and bosom
Fondly straining to her own;
Oft her pallid lips imprinting
On each wound of her dear Son;
Till at last, in swoons of anguish,
Sense and consciousness are gone.

4 Gentle Mother, we beseech thee,
By thy tears and troubles sore,

By the death of thy dear offspring,
  By the bloody wounds He bore ;
Touch our hearts with that true sorrow
  Which afflicted thee of yore.

5 To the Father everlasting,
  And the Son, who reigns on high,
With the coeternal Spirit,
  Trinity in Unity,
Be salvation, honour, blessing,
  Now and through eternity.

---

41. *The Assumption.*

1 Sing, sing, ye Angel bands,
  All beautiful and bright ;
For higher still, and higher,
  Through fields of starry light,
Mary, your Queen, ascends,
  Like the sweet moon at night.

2 A fairer flower than she
  On earth hath never been ;
And, save the throne of God,
  Your heavens have never seen .
A wonder half so bright
  As your ascending Queen.

3 O happy Angels ! look,
  How beautiful she is !
See ! Jesus bears her up,
  Her hand is locked in His ;
O who can tell the height
  Of that fair Mother's bliss ?

4 And shall I lose thee then,
    Lose my sweet right to thee?
Ah, no! the Angels' Queen
    Man's mother still will be;
And thou, upon thy throne,
    Wilt keep thy love for me.

5 On, then, dear Pageant, on!
    Sweet music breathes around;
And love, like dew, distils
    On hearts in rapture bound;
The Queen of heaven goes up
    To be proclaimed and crowned!

6 On through the countless stars
    Proceeds the bright array;
And Love Divine comes forth
    To light her on her way,
Through the short gloom of night
    Into celestial day.

7 The Eternal Father calls
    His daughter to be blessed;
The Son His maiden-mother
    Woos unto His breast;
The Holy Ghost His spouse
    Beckons into her rest.

8 Swifter and swifter grows
    That marvellous flight of love,
As though her heart were drawn
    More vehemently above;
While jubilant Angels part
    A pathway for the Dove!

9 Hark! Hark! through highest heaven
    What sounds of mystic mirth!
Mary, by God proclaimed
    Queen of Immaculate birth
And diademed with stars,
    The lowliest of the earth!

10 See! see! the Eternal Hands
    Put on her radiant crown,
And the sweet Majesty
    Of Mercy, sitteth down
For ever and for ever
    On her predestined throne!

---

42. *The Triumph of the Blessed Virgin.*

1 Queen of the skies, triumphant Queen!
Each clime and age, a glad tribute yielding
To thee, their crowned triumphant Queen,
With heart and voice in glad accents sing. } CHORUS.
    Love shall still inspire
    Hearts with sacred fire,
    Love shall still inspire
    Hymns of praise to thee.
And our voices never tire
While we sing with tuneful glee,
    Repeat.—Queen of the skies, &c.

2 Sing on this day, this sacred day
All Mary's gifts, all her matchless power;
Sing on this day, this sacred day
Praises and hymns through each gladsome hour.

On her love relying
We her children kneeling
On her bosom leaning
At her hands receive
Endless stores of grace and blessing
All a mother's love can give.
    Repeat.—Queen of the skies, &c.

3 Let the sweet spell of Mary's name
Dwell in our hearts, in our mem'ries linger,
Let the sweet spell of Mary's name
Still be the joy of all who love her.
    Then let Saints and Angels,
    Seraphs and Archangels,
    Men of every country,
    Vie in praise and love;
Sing with joy their mother's mercy
Never from her presence rove.
    Repeat.—Queen of the skies, &c.

4 Keep in thy heart thy children's names,
Stamp on their own thy maternal likeness,
Teach them to own thy tender claims,
Teach them thy Son to love and to bless.
    Watch over their childhood,
    Guide them in their manhood,
    Keep them pure and holy
    Safe under thy wing.
And when life is ebbing slowly
Let them still with fervour sing.
    Repeat.—Queen of the skies, &c.

43. *Hail, Queen of Heaven.*

1 Hail, Queen of Heav'n, the ocean star,
　Guide of the wand'rer here below !
Thrown on life's surge we claim thy care,
　Save us from peril and from woe.
　　　　Mother of Christ, star of the sea,
　　　　Pray for the wanderer, pray for me.

2 O gentle, chaste, and spotless maid,
　We sinners make our prayers through thee,
Remind thy Son that He has paid
　The price of our iniquity.
　　　　Virgin most pure, star of the sea,
　　　　Pray for the sinner, pray for me.

3 Sojourners in this vale of tears,
　To thee, blest advocate, we cry,
Pity our sorrows, calm our fears,
　And soothe with hope our misery.
　　　　Refuge in grief, star of the sea,
　　　　Pray for the mourner, pray for me.

4 And while, to Him who reigns above,
　In Godhead One, in Persons Three,
The source of life, of grace, of love,
　Homage we pay on bended knee ;
　　　　Do thou, bright Queen, star of the sea,
　　　　Pray for thy children, pray for me.

———

44. *Daily, daily sing to Mary.*

1 Daily, daily sing to Mary :
　Sing, my soul, her praises due

All her feasts, her actions worship,
  With the heart's devotion true.
Lost in wond'ring contemplation,
  Be her Majesty confest:
Call her Mother, call her Virgin,
  Happy Mother, Virgin blest.

2 She is mighty to deliver;
    Call her, trust her lovingly:
  When the tempest rages round thee,
    She will calm the troubled sea.
  Gifts of Heaven she has given,
    Noble lady! to our race:
  She the Queen, who decks her subjects
    With the light of God's own grace.

3 Sing, my tongue, the Virgin's trophies,
    Who for us her Maker bore:
  For the curse of old inflicted,
    Peace and blessing to restore.
  Sing in songs of praise unending,
    Sing the world's majestic Queen,
  Weary not, nor faint in telling,
    All the gifts she gives to men.

---

45. *The Praises of Mary.*

1 Holy Queen! we bend before thee,
    Queen of purity divine!
  Make us love thee, we implore thee
    Make us truly to be thine.

CHORUS.

Teach, oh teach us, Holy Mother
How to conquer ev'ry sin;
How to love and help each other;
How the prize of life to win.

2 Thou to whom a Child was given
Greater than the sons of men,
Coming down from highest heaven
To create the world again.
Chorus.—Teach, oh teach us, &c.

3 O, by that Almighty Maker,
Whom thyself a Virgin bore!
O, by thy supreme Creator,
Link'd with thee for evermore!
Chorus.—Teach, oh teach us, &c.

4 By the hope thy name inspires!
By our doom reversed through thee:
Help us, Queen of Angel choirs!
To a blest eternity!
Chorus.—Teach, oh teach us, &c.

46. *Look down, O Mother Mary.*
(From St. Alphonso.)

1 Look down, O Mother Mary!
From thy bright throne above;
Cast down upon thy children
One only glance of love.

And if a heart so tender
With pity flows not o'er,

Then turn away, O Mother !
And look on us no more.
    Repeat.—Look down, &c.

2 See how ingrate and guilty
    We stand before thy Son ;
His loving heart reproaches
    The evil we have done.

But if thou wilt appease Him,
    Speak for us but one word ;
Thou only canst obtain us
    The pardon of our Lord.
    Repeat.—Look down, &c.

3 O Mary, dearest Mother !
    If thou wouldst have us live,
Say that we are thy children,
    And then He will forgive.

Our sins make us unworthy
    That title still to bear,
But thou art still our Mother !
    Then show a mother's care.
    Repeat.—Look down, &c.

4 Open to us thy mantle,
    There stay we without fear ;
What evil can befall us
    If, Mother, thou art near ?

O sweetest, dearest Mother !
    Thy sinful children save ;
Look down on us with pity,
    Who thy protection crave.
    Repeat.—Look down, &c.

47. *Mother of Mercy.*

Repeat the last line of every verse.

1 Mother of Mercy! day by day
     My love for thee grows more and more
  Thy gifts are strewn upon my way,
     Like sands upon the great sea shore.

2 Though poverty, and work, and woe
     The masters of my life may be,
  When times are worst, who does not know
     Darkness is light, with love of thee?

3 But scornful men have coldly said
     Thy love was leading me from God;
  And yet in this I did but tread
     The very path my Saviour trod.

4 They know but little of thy worth
     Who speak these heartless words to me;
  For what did Jesus love on earth
     One half so tenderly as thee?

5 Get me the grace to love thee more
     Jesus will give if thou wilt plead;
  And, Mother! when life's cares are o'er,
     O I shall love thee then indeed!

6 Jesus, when His three hours were run,
     Bequeath'd thee from the cross to me;
  And O! how can I love thy Son,
     Sweet Mother! if I love not thee?

48. *The Sailor's Hymn.*

1   Mary Mother!
Shield us through life!
    Protect us from
The ocean's strife.

CHORUS.

Calm the wild sea,
  Bid tempests cease;
Through thee we reach } Repeat.
  The shore in peace. }

2   Star of the main
Beneath thy veil
    Clinging to thee
We safely sail.
        Chorus.—Calm the wild, &c.

3   O mother dear
O virgin blest;
    Our footsteps guide
Till death's long rest.
        Chorus.—Calm the wild, &c.

4   Sweet morning star,
When life is o'er,
    Then land us on
Th' eternal shore.
        Chorus.—Calm the wild, &c.

49. *Mother Mary.*

1 I shall see this cherished Mother,
   This sweet hope beats in my heart;
Who can tell her love and goodness?
   In her presence griefs depart.

CHORUS.

   Mother Mary !
   This dark night
   Is lit from heaven } Repeat.
   With thy light.

2 All her love has flowed around me,
   I have ever been her child,
And my sorrow for her absence
   Deepens in this desert wild.
     Chorus.—Mother Mary, &c.

3 All my joy is loving Mary,
   And the light of her sweet name
Falling in a rain of glory,
   Crowns us with its ambient flame.
     Chorus.—Mother Mary, &c.

4 When I see my Mother's image
   Then my thoughts are ever bold,
Fashioning some dim resemblance
   Of her loveliness untold.
     Chorus.—Mother Mary, &c.

5 Dreary days of Mary's absence !
  Dark days without Mary's light !
Yet will come the wished-for morning
O'er the threshold of the night.
    Chorus.—Mother Mary, &c.

6 Though we see her not, her presence
  Hangeth round us evermore :
In her star-crowned love she dwelleth—
Past the waves—upon the shore.
    Chorus.—Mother Mary, &c.

7 Mother Mary, help thy children !
  We are evermore thine own !
Watch us, shield us in this sorrow
Sitting on thy royal throne.
    Chorus.—Mother Mary, &c.

---

50. *Consecration to the Blessed Virgin Mary.*

1 I hear thy false sweet voice, deceitful world,
Vain are thy lures and vain thy artful charms ;
True to my Queen, I own no rule but hers,
My hope, my home, is in my mother's arms ;
  Her badge I wear, I own her sway,
  I fear no foes on the battle day.

CHORUS.

Queen of the sky, mother blest and belov'd,
Turn on us thine eyes, see we hasten to thee,
Lo ! at thy feet, O dear mother, we swear,
True children of Mary for ever to be. (*3 times.*)

2 Let sinful men exult in worldly joys,
  Short is their bliss, short-lived its transient
     glow;
  Wild shouts of glee and bursts of laughter loud
  Serve but to hide the heart's deep-seated woe;
    But grief ensues, remorse awakes,
    And peace the guilty soul forsakes.
     Chorus.—Queen of the sky, &c.

3 Then bring fresh wreaths, and crown my head
    with flowers;
  " Life is a feast," the reckless sinner cries,
  " Let pleasures spring each day beneath my
    feet,"
  But pleasures end, and soon the sinner dies;
    Oh! what shall be that sinner's fate
    Who thinks of death and hell too late!
     Chorus.—Queen of the sky, &c.

----

51. *To our Blessed Lady, for the Souls in*
Purgatory.

1 O turn to Jesus, Mother, turn,
  And call Him by His tenderest names;
  Pray for the holy souls that burn
  This hour among the cleansing flames.

  Ah! they have fought a gallant fight;
  In death's cold arms they persevered;
  And after life's uncheery night
  The harbour of their rest is neared.

5

2 In pains beyond all earthly pains,
Favourites of Jesus! there they lie,
Letting the fire wear out their stains,
And worshipping God's purity.

Spouses of Christ they are, for He
Was wedded to them by His Blood;
And angels o'er their destiny
In wondering adoration brood.

3 They are the children of thy tears;
Then hasten, Mother! to their aid;
In pity think each hour appears
An age while glory is delayed.

See, how they bound amid their fires,
While pain and love their spirits fill;
Then with self-crucified desires
Utter sweet murmurs and lie still.

4 O Mary! let thy Son no more
His lingering spouses thus expect;
God's children to their God restore,
And to the Spirit His elect.

Pray then, as thou hast ever prayed;
Angels and souls all look to thee;
God waits thy prayers, for He hath made
Those prayers His law of charity.

---

52. *Evening Hymn to our Blessed Lady.*

1 Bright Queen of Heaven,
   Virgin most fair,
  Mary most gentle,
   List to our prayer.

Mother protect us,
   Aid to us bring,
Sweetly enfold us
   'Neath shelt'ring wing.

2 Star of the ocean,
   Shedding soft light,
Solace in sorrow,
   Rest 'mid the night;
Send in our slumbers
   Peace from above,
Shine on us ever,
   Bright star of love.

3 Tho' night be lonely
   Why should we fear,
While thy soft gleaming
   Shineth so near,
Leading us gently
   'Mid darkling gloom,
Beck'ning us onwards,
   To our true home?

4 Soon may the morrow
   Of bright endless day,
Chase the drear visions
   Of dark night away;
Waft our lone spirits
   To heaven's bright shore,
Where we may love thee
   And rest evermore.

IV. ST. JOSEPH.

53. *Hail! holy Joseph.*

1 Hail! holy Joseph, hail!
  Husband of Mary, hail!
Chaste as the lily flower
  In Eden's peaceful vale.

2 Hail! holy Joseph, hail!
  Father of Christ esteemed!
Father be thou to those
  Thy Foster-Son redeemed.

3 Hail! holy Joseph, hail!
  Prince of the house of God,
May His best graces be
  By thy sweet hands bestowed.

4 Hail! holy Joseph, hail!
  Comrade of angels, hail!
Cheer thou the hearts that faint,
  And guide the steps that fail.

5 Hail! holy Joseph, hail!
  God's choice wert thou alone;
To thee the Word made flesh
  Was subject as a Son.

6 Hail! holy Joseph, hail!
  Teach us our flesh to tame;
And, Mary, keep the hearts
  That love thy husband's name.

7 Mother of Jesus! bless,
   And bless, ye saints on high,
All meek and simple souls
   That to Saint Joseph cry.

---

54. *Patronage of St. Joseph.*

1 There are many saints above,
   Who love us with true love,
Many angels ever nigh;
   But, Joseph! none there be,
   O none that love like thee—
Dearest of Saints! be near us when we die.

2 Thou wert guardian of our Lord,
   Foster-father of the Word,
Who in thine arms did lie;
   If we His brothers be,
   We are foster-sons to thee—
Dearest of Saints! be near us when we die.

3 Thou wert Mary's earthly guide,
   For ever at her side,
Oh, for her sake hear our cry;
   For we follow in thy way,
   Loving Mary as we may—
Dearest of Saints! be near us when we die.

4 Thou to Mary's virgin love
  Wert the image of the Dove,
Who was her spouse on high ;
  Bring us gifts from Him, dear saint !
  Bring us comfort when we faint—
Dearest of saints ! be near us when we die.

5 Sadly o'er the desert sands,
  Into Egypt's darksome lands,
As an exile didst thou fly ;
  And we are exiles too,
  With a world to travel through—
Dearest of saints ! be near us when we die.

6 When thy gentle years were run,
  On the bosom of thy Son,
Like an infant didst thou lie ;
  Oh by thy happy death,
  In the tranquil Nazareth—
Dearest of saints ! be near us when we die.

———

55. *St. Joseph to the Infant Jesus.*
(From St. Alphonso.)

1 " Jesus ! let me call thee son,
    Since Thou dost call me father ;
How I love Thee, sweetest One !
    My God and son together ;"

CHORUS.

Blessed St. Joseph ! to thee do we pray
Offer our hearts to thy Jesus to-day,} Repeat.

2 "As my God, I Thee adore,
    And as my Son, embrace Thee;
Let me love Thee more and more,
    And in my bosom place Thee."
           Chorus.—Blessed St. Joseph, &c.

3 " Since Thy guardian I must be,
    My treasure I will make Thee;
Do not Thou abandon me,
    And I will ne'er forsake Thee."
           Chorus.—Blessed St. Joseph, &c.

4 "All my love henceforth is Thine,
    My very life I proffer;
And my heart no more is mine,
    For all I am I offer."
           Chorus.—Blessed St. Joseph, &c.

5 " Since to share Thy presence sweet
    To choose me here Thou deignest;
Shall we not in heaven meet,
    Where Thou for ever reignest?"
           Chorus.—Blessed St. Joseph, &c.

———

V. THE HOLY FAMILY.

56. *'Praise to Jesus, Joseph, Mary.'*

1 Praise, praise to Jesus, Joseph, Mary,
    The Three on earth most like the Three in
      heaven!

Praise, praise to Jesus, Joseph, Mary,
To whom these Heavenly Likenesses were
given!
Come Christians, come, sweet anthems
weaving,
Come, young and old, come, gay or
grieving!

CHORUS.

Come Christians, come, sweet anthems
weaving,
Come, young and old, come, gay or
grieving!
Praise, praise with me
Adoring and believing
God's Family, God's Holy Family! } Repeat.

2 'Mid Nazareth's sequestered mountains
How lovely was the household of the Three!
And by the desert's crystal fountains
What secret wonders did not Angels see.
Come Christians, come, &c. (as ver. 1.)
Chorus.—Come Christians, come, &c.

3 Then by the dark Egyptian river,
Joseph, the Mother, and the marvellous
Child,
Heard the chill night-wind softly quiver
In the tall palms or o'er the sandfields wild.
Come Christians, come, &c. (as ver. 1.)
Chorus.—Come Christians, come, &c

4 Sweet Family! swift years are speeding;
    Thrice ten hath passed o'er Nazareth's secret
       home:
Poor weary world! it lies all bleeding;
    Why should it wait? Why should not Jesus
      come?
        Come Christians, come, &c. (as ver. 1.)
          Chorus.—Come Christians, come, &c.

5 Sweet Family! thy charms detain Him:
    Thou savest Him from an untimely woe:
From men that would too soon have slain Him
He hides in thee, God's paradise below!
        Come Christians, come, &c. (as ver. 1.)
          Chorus.—Come Christians, come, &c.

6 O House of Nazareth! Earth's Heaven!
    Our households now are hallowed all by thee!
All blessings come, all gifts are given,
    Because of thy dear earthly Trinity!
        Come Christians, come, &c. (as ver. 1.)
          Chorus.—Come Christians, come, &c.

7 Sing to the Three with jubilation!
    Husbands and wives, parents and children
      sing!
Sing to the House from which Salvation
    Flows o'er your homes as from a hidden
      spring!
        Come Christians, come, &c. (as ver. 1.)
          Chorus.—Come Christians, come, &c.

8 Now praise, O praise the sinless Mother,
　　Praise to that household's gentle Master be ;
And with the Child, whom we call Brother,
　　O weep for joy of that dear Family !
　　　Come Christians, come, &c. (as ver. 1.)
　　　　Chorus.—Come Christians, come, &c.

57.　*The Banner of the Holy Family.*

CHORUS.

Let us fight ! for God let us fight !
Come let us throng round our Banner !
Wave it high now our Glorious Banner ;
See how it glistens in the light :
O heart of Joseph ! O heart of Mary !
Whose Heart with yours shines out so bright?
It is our Jesus! it is our Saviour,
Our Lord, our Leader in the fight !

1 Hark the sound of the fight hath gone forth,
　　And we must not tarry at home ;
For our Lord from the South and the North
　　Has commanded His soldiers to come.
　　　　　Chorus.—Let us fight, &c.

2 We must on with our Banner unfurled :
　　We must on : 'tis Jesus who leads :
We must hasten to conquer the world,
　　With the Sign of the Lamb who bleeds.
　　　　　Chorus.—Let us fight, &c.

3 We must stand to our colours like men:
    Our Lord is a Leader to love:
For the wounded He heals; and the slain
    He crowns in His city above.
              Chorus.—Let us fight, &c.

4 We must march to the battle with speed:
    Upon earth our one duty is strife:
O blest are the soldiers who bleed
    For the Saviour who died to give life.
              Chorus.—Let us fight, &c.

5 There are Three up in Heaven above—
    There are Three upon earth below:
And Theirs is the Standard we love—
    And Theirs the one watchword we know.
              Chorus.—Let us fight, &c.

6 Let us sing the new song of the Lamb—
    Let us sing round our Banner so brave:
Let us sing of that beautiful Blood
    Which was shed to redeem and to save.
              Chorus.—Let us fight, &c.

---

58. *Brightly gleams our Banner!*

1 Brightly gleams our banner,
    Pointing to the sky,
Waving wand'rers onwards,
    To their home on high.

Hail. O holy banner,
  Gladly thus we pray;
And with hearts united,
  Take our heavenward way.

  Brightly gleams our banner,
    Pointing to the sky,
  Waving wand'rers onwards,
    To their home on high.

2 Hail! sweet Jesus! Master!
    Round Thy sacred feet,
  Now, with hearts rejoicing
    See Thy children meet.
  Long, alas, we've left Thee,
    Straying far away;
  But once more we enter
    On the " narrow way."
        Chorus.—Brightly gleams, &c.

3 Mary, Mother, Ave!
    Israel's lily hail!
  Comfort of thy children
    In this sinful vale.
  'Mid life's surging ocean,
    Whither shall we flee,
  Save, O stainless Virgin,
    Mother, unto thee?
        Chorus.—Brightly gleams, &c.

4 Ave! Joseph! Ave!
   Chaste and spotless flower;
Cast thy mantle o'er us
   At death's solemn hour.
Be our Father ever,
   Joseph, meek and mild;
Husband of our Mother,
   Keeper of her Child.
        Chorus.—Brightly gleams, &c.

5 Jesus! Mary! Joseph!
   Sweet and holy Three;
List the praise we pay you
   On our bended knee.
May we sing your glory
   In glad realms above;
Bound for ever to you,
   By the bonds of love.
        Chorus.—Brightly gleams, &c.

---

59. *'Happy we who thus united.'*

1 Happy we, who thus united
   Join in cheerful melody,
Praising Jesus, Mary, Joseph,
   In the " Holy Family."

CHORUS.

Jesus, Mary, Joseph. help us,
   That we ever true may be
To the promises that bind us
   To the " Holy Family."

2 Jesus, whose Almighty bidding
    All created things fulfil,
Lives on earth in meek subjection
    To His earthly parent's will.

CHORUS.

Sweetest Infant! make us patient
    And obedient for Thy sake ;
Teach us to be chaste and gentle,
    All our stormy passions break.

3 Mary ! thou alone wert chosen
    To be Mother of thy Lord :
Thou didst guide the early footsteps
    Of the Great Incarnate Word.

CHORUS.

Dearest Mother ! make us humble,
    For thy Son will take His rest
In the poor and lowly dwelling
    Of an humble sinner's breast.

4 Joseph ! thou wert called the Father
    Of thy Maker and thy Lord,
Thine it was to save thy Saviour
    From the cruel Herod's sword.

CHORUS.

Suffer us to call thee Father,
    Shew to us a Father's love ;
Lead us safe through every danger
    Till we meet in heaven above.

60. *One Heart, one Soul have Brothers.*

CHORUS.

One Heart, one Soul have Brothers,
By love's eternal might,
Of all and each they're lovers,
Who walk in Heaven's sight.

1 O sweet the tie of Brother,
In holy bondage bound,
As sons of one same mother,
In true affection found.
Chorus.—One Heart, &c.

2 Nor jarring words of anger,
Nor looks unkind we know,
Nor paths which souls endanger
And lead to endless woe.
Chorus.—One Heart, &c.

3 Our union is all holy,
By God's own blessing blest,
In spirits meek and lowly
That seek a heav'nly rest.
Chorus.—One Heart, &c.

4 Then let us all remember
Pure Charity's sweet ways,
And be in kindness tender,
True Brothers all our days.
Chorus.—One Heart, &c.

61. *All for Jesus, Mary, and Joseph.*

1 Let those who seek the world to please,
Do all for honour, wealth, and ease;
But in the Holy Family,
A nobler motive far, have we.

CHORUS.

Living, we will say
Joyfully each day:
All for Jesus, Mary, Joseph!
Dying, we will cry
Till our latest sigh,
All for Jesus, Mary, Joseph!

2 O wicked world! we know thee well,
Thy works and maxims lead to hell:
We were thy slaves, but now are free,
We serve the Holy Family.
    Chorus.—Living, we will say, &c.

3 What matter tho' we sometimes bear
A little suffering, toil, and care;
We serve a good and bounteous Lord,
And Heav'n will soon be our reward.
    Chorus.—Living, we will say, &c.

4 What tho' despised and poor we be,
We're like the Holy Family:
If They could poverty endure,
We should be proud to be as poor.
    Chorus.—Living, we will say, &c.

5 And when this wretched life is past,
   And every moment seems the last,
   Oh then, the Holy Family
   Our sweetest hope in death will be!

Living, we will say,
Joyfully each day,
All for Jesus, Mary, Joseph!
And when death is nigh,
Still our hearts will cry,
All for Jesus, Mary, Joseph!

VI. THE ANGELS AND SAINTS.

62. *Dear Angel, ever at my side.*

1 Dear angel! ever at my side,
   How loving must thou be,
   To leave thy home in heaven to guard
   A guilty wretch like me.

Thy beautiful and shining face
I see not, though so near;
The sweetness of thy soft low voice
I am too deaf to hear.

3 I cannot feel thee touch my hand
   With pressure light and mild,
   To check me, as my mother did
   When I was but a child.

4 But I have felt thee in my thoughts
   Fighting with sin for me;
And when my heart loves God, I know,
   The sweetness is from thee.

5 And when, dear Spirit! I kneel down
   Morning and night, to prayer,
Something there is within my heart
   Which tells me thou art there.

6 Yes! when I pray, thou prayest too—
   Thy prayer is all for me;
But when I sleep, thou sleepest not,
   But watchest patiently.

7 But most of all I feel thee near,
   When from the good priest's feet,
I go absolved, in fearless love
   Fresh toils and cares to meet.

8 And thou in life's last hour wilt bring
   A fresh supply of grace,
And afterwards wilt let me kiss
   Thy beautiful bright face.

9 Ah me! how lovely they must be
   Whom God has glorified!
Yet one of them, O sweetest thought!
   Is ever at my side.

10 Then for thy sake, dear Angel! now
   More humble will I be:
But I am weak, and when I fall,
   O weary not for me.

11 O weary not, but love me still,
    For Mary's sake, thy Queen ;
  She never tired of me, though I,
    Her worst of sons have been.

12 She will reward thee with a smile ;
    Thou know'st what it is worth !
  For Mary's smiles each day convert
    The hardest hearts on earth.

13 Then love me, love me, angel dear !
    And I will love thee more !
  And help me when my soul is cast
    Upon the eternal shore.

63. *St. Anne.*

1 O Anne ! thou hadst lived through those long
    dreary years,
  When childlessness hung o'er thy home like
    a blight.
  But angels, dear mother ! were counting thy
    tears,
    And thy patience, like Job's, had been dear
    in God's sight.

2 Thou wert meek when they scorned thee ; thy
    rest was in prayer ;
  Thy sorrow was sharp, yet its sharpness was

When those that were round thee gave way to
    despair,
  Thy faith was more certain, thy trust more
    complete.

3 O the vision of thee in thy lone mountain
    home,
  With thy calm broken heart so heart-break-
    ing to see,
In those dark after-years to thy daughter might
    come,
  And the great Queen of sorrows learn some-
    thing from thee.

4 But joy comes at length to all hearts that
    believed
  And the sighs of the saints must at last end
    in song ;
The best gifts of God fall to those who have
    grieved,
  And His love is the stronger for waiting so
    long.

5 O blest be the day, when old earth bore its
    fruit,
  The fairest of daughters it ever had seen,
In the village that lies at the white mountain
    foot,
  And the angels sang songs to the young
    Nazarene.

6 'Mid the carols of shepherds, the bleating of
    sheep,
    The joy of that birth, blessed Anne! came to
    thee,
When the fruits were grown golden, the grapes
    blushing deep,
    In the fields and the orchards of green Gali-
    lee!

7 Since creation, was ever such gladness as thine,
    To whom God's chosen mother, as daughter
    was given?
O her beautiful eyes, dearest Anne! how they
    shine,
    And the sound of her voice is like music from
    Heaven.

8 Why was it thy heart did not break with excess
    Of a joy that was harder than sorrow to
    bear?
Perchance had thine earlier sorrows been less,
    Thou couldst not have lived with a vision so
    fair!

9 Like a presence of God in thy home's hallowed
    bound,
    Like a pageant of heaven all day was she
    seen;
O didst thou not see how the angels thronged
    round
    All amazed at the sight of their infantine
    Queen?

10 She was crowned, even then, like a creature
       apart,
     The child God had called to be mother and
       maid !
    Didst thou watch how the fountains of blood in
       her heart,
     Like the fountains. in Sion, incessantly
       played ?

11 O Anne ! from that blood the Creator will take
     The flesh that shall save the lost tribes of our
       race ;
    And His wonderful love the Eternal will slake
     At thy child's sinless heart, at those fountains
       of grace !

12 O Anne ! joyous saint ! what a life didst thou
       live,
     What an unbroken brightness of innocent
       bliss !
    Every touch of thy child a fresh rapture could
       give,
     And oh ! didst thou not kneel ere thou daredst
       to kiss ?

13 And we too, glad Mother, are gay with thy
       mirth ;
     For thy child, like a sunbeam lies over our
       lives ;
    There is brightness and goodness all over the
       earth
     For the souls Mary welcomes and Jesus for-
       gives.

14 Yes! gladness makes holy the poor heart of
    man;
  It lightens life's sorrows, it softens its smarts;
  O be with thy children, then, dearest St.
    Anne!
  For Mary, thy child, is the joy of our hearts!

---

64. *Spotless Anna! Juda's Glory!*

CHORUS.
Gather'd round thy sacred banner,
  ·In the Church that bears thy name,*
Mary's Mother! gracious Anna!
  We thy grace and favour claim.

1 Spotless Anna! Juda's glory!
  Through the Church from East to West,
Every tongue proclaims thy praises,
  Holy Mary's mother blest!
     Chorus.—Gather'd round, &c.

2 Saintly Kings and priestly Sires
  Blended in thy sacred line;
Thou in virtue, all before thee
  Didst excel by grace divine.
     Chorus.—Gather'd round, &c.

3 Linked in bonds of purest wedlock,
  Thine it was for us to bear,
By the favour of High Heaven,
  Our eternal Virgin Star.
     Chorus —Gather'd round, &c.

* In Churches not dedicated to St. Anne,
  Here in homage of thy name.

4 From thy stem in beauty budded
   Ancient Jesse's mystic rod;
Earth from thee received the Mother
   Of th' Almighty Son of God.
        Chorus.—Gather'd round, &c.

5 All the human race benighted
   In the depths of darkness lay ;
When in Anne, it saw the dawning
   Of the long expected day.
        Chorus.—Gather'd round, &c.

6 Honour, glory, virtue, merit,
   Be to Thee, O Virgin's Son !
With the Father and the Spirit,
   While eternal ages run.
        Chorus.—Gather'd round, &c.

————

65. *Saint Patrick.*

1 On wings of holy charity
   To Erin's coast Saint Patrick came,
To curb the devil's tyranny
   And spread the love of Jesu's name.

CHORUS.

The Faith is firm in Erin's land,
   And Patrick dear to Irish hearts ;
Though heresy has raised her brand ;
   And struck her sons with Satan's darts.} Repeat.

2 Through ages long of gloomy night
  Our Fathers in fell bondage lay,
When Patrick brought the gospel's light,
  To light in truth our heav'nward way.
          Chorus.—The Faith is firm, &c.

3 Then by celestial doctrine taught
  To Faith and Hope, was Erin turned:
The flame of Love, her children caught,
  And Peter's chair, their Faith confirmed.
          Chorus.—The Faith is firm, &c.

4 A land of Saints was Erin soon,
  And Eden's peace was there renewed,
The toad and viper knew their doom
  And fled, where Patrick's steps pursued.
          Chorus.—The Faith is firm, &c.

5 Still Patrick pray that sin may fly
  From every Irish heart and home,
And those who love to own thee nigh
  In lawless ways may never roam.
          Chorus.—The Faith is firm, &c

---

66. *St. Vincent of Paul.*

CHORUS.

O Blessed Father! sent by God,
  His mercy to dispense,
Thy hand is out o'er all the earth
  Like God's own providence.

1 There is no grief or care of men
   Thou dost not own for thine,
No broken heart thou dost not fill
   With mercy's oil and wine.
        Chorus.—O Blessed Father! &c.

2 Thy miracles are works of love;
   Thy greatest is to make
Room in a day, for toils that weeks
   In other men would take.
        Chorus.—O Blessed Father! &c.

3 All cries of suffering through the earth
   Upon thy mercy call,
As though thou wert, like God Himself,
   A father unto all.
        Chorus.—O Blessed Father! &c.

4 Dear Saint, not in the wilderness
   Thy fragrant virtues bloom,
But in the city's crowded haunts,
   The alley's cheerless gloom:
        Chorus.—O Blessed Father! &c.

5 The father of the childless old,
   The lonesome widow's stay,
The gladness of the orphan groups
   Out in the streets at play.
        Chorus.—O Blessed Father! &c.

6 Yet not unto the towns confined
   The gifts thy mercy gave,
The gospel to the villager,
   His freedom to the slave.
        Chorus.—O Blessed Father! &c.

7 So for the sake of timid souls,
  And love of winning ways,
Thou didst against hard-hearted schools
  Thy gentle protest raise.
        Chorus.—O Blessed Father ! &c.

8 For charity anointed thee
  O'er want, and woe, and pain ;
And she hath crowned thee emperor
  Of all her wide domain.
        Chorus.—O Blessed Father ! &c

------

67. *To St. Alphonsus.*

Hark ! Angelic songs resounding
  Thro' the happy courts of Heaven !
For the triumph of Alphonsus
  Endless praise to God is given.

CHORUS.

Saint Alphonsus ! Holy Patron
  Of our Confraternity,
Let thy children sing thy praises
  In a blest eternity.

2 See Alphonsus silent kneeling,
  Wrapt in loving ecstasy,
At the Altar where his Jesus
  Hides in love His majesty.

CHORUS.

Saint Alphonsus! dearest Father!
  Would our hearts were like to thine;
Make us share thy deep devotion
  To this Sacrament divine.

3 By the crib where Jesus, trembling,
    Lies upon a little straw,
  See Alphonsus lowly bending
    Lost in tenderness and awe.

CHORUS.

Blessed Father! make thy children
  Love the Babe of Bethlehem,
Till with thee we see His glory
  In the New Jerusalem.

4 Lost in loving contemplation
    Of the Passion of his Lord,
  See Alphonsus, pierced with anguish,
    Shares in Mary's bitter sword.

CHORUS.

Saint Alphonsus! our offences
  Nailed thy Jesus to the wood,
Pray that they may now be cancelled
  By His sweet and saving blood.

---

68. *Saint Aloysius Gonzaga,*

Patron of Youth.

1 Angelic youth! at whose blest birth
  Bright choirs of heavenly spirits thronged;

How great the day which gave to earth
A treasure that to heaven belonged !

CHORUS.

Patron of youth who pure hast known,
The dangers that beset our way, .
We fear the world to walk alone,
Let thy sweet name support and stay.] Repeat.

2 O happy youth, from thy first hour,
Thy steps e'er were to heaven bound,
Thou ne'er didst yield to demon power,
Nor fall 'neath sin which raged around.
   Chorus.—Patron of youth, &c.

3 Thy guileless tongue and gentle heart
From Jesus' love was never riven,
In things of earth thou hadst no part,
For all thy thoughts were set on heaven.
   Chorus.—Patron of youth, &c.

4 From dewy morn till evening fair,
From Vespers' toll till break of day,
Our enemies their toils prepare,
And seek to make our souls their prey.
   Chorus.—Patron of youth, &c.

5 Oh be our guide, for thou wert pure,
And we are stained with many a sin ;
Without, life's ills we scarce endure,
Alas! how cold and dark within.
   Chorus.—Patron of youth, &c.

6 Life's morn is past, the sky grows dark,
And clouds forebode a troubled sea,
The waves are swelling round our bark,
It may not speed unblest by thee.
   Chorus.—Patron of youth, &c.

7 Thro' Christ's sweet love, oh pray for those
For whom He died upon the tree ;
Thro' love thy soul has gained repose,
Thro' love we hope to follow thee.
   Chorus.—Patron of youth, &c.

69. *The Apostles.*

1 The Lord's eternal gifts,
  Th' Apostles' mighty praise,
Their victories, and high reward,
  Sing we in joyful lays.

2 Lords of the Churches they ;
  Triumphant chiefs of war ;
Brave Soldiers of the Heavenly Court ;
  True lights for evermore.

3 Theirs was the saints high faith
  And quenchless hope's pure glow ;
And perfect charity, which laid
  The world's fell tyrant low.

4 In them the Father shone ;
  In them the Son o'ercame ;
In them the Holy Spirit wrought ;
  And filled their hearts with flame.

5　　To God, the Father, Son,
　　　And Spirit, glory be ;
　As was, and is, and shall be so,
　　　Through all eternity.

———

70.　*A Martyr or Confessor.*

Repeat the last line of each verse.

1 O Thou the Martyrs' glorious King!
　　Of Confessors the crown and prize !
　Who dost to joys celestial bring
　　Those who the joys of earth despise.

2 By all the praise Thy saints have won ;
　　By all their pains in days gone by ;
　By all the deeds which they have done ;
　　Hear Thou Thy suppliant people's cry.

3 Thou dost amid Thy soldiers fight ;
　　And all Thy children's guilt forgive ;
　May we find mercy in Thy sight,
　　And in Thy sacred presence live.

4 To God the Father glory be,
　　And to His sole-begotten Son ;
　The same, O Holy Ghost, to Thee !
　　While everlasting ages run.

71. *Holy Virgins.*

Repeat the last line of each verse.

1 Thou crown of all the Virgin choir !
   That holy Mother's Virgin Son !
 Who is, alone of womankind,
   Mother and Virgin both in one !

2 Encircled by thy virgin band,
   Amid the lilies Thou art found ;
 For Thy pure brides with lavish hand
   Scattering immortal graces round.

3 And still, wherever Thou dost bend
   Thy lovely steps, O glorious King,
 Virgins upon Thy steps attend,
   And hymns to Thy high glory sing.

4 Keep us, O Purity divine,
   From every least corruption free ;
 Our every sense from sin refine,
   And purify our souls for Thee.

5 To God the Father and the Son,
   All honour, glory, praise be given ;
 With Thee O holy Paraclete !
   Henceforth by all in earth and heaven.

---

72. *All Saints.*

" Placare, Christe, Servulis."

Repeat the last line of each verse,

1 O Jesus, let Thy anger cease :
 Thy Virgin Mother, for our peace,

At Thy tribunal pleading stands,
And mercy earnestly demands.

2 And ye, O Angels, who in Nine
Distinguish'd Orders glorious shine,
Preserve our minds, our hearts, our wills,
From present, past, and future ills.

3 Ye Prophets and Apostles plead
Before our Judge, and intercede
For sinners; that by tears unfeign'd
His pardoning grace may be obtain'd.

4 Ye crimson troop of Martyrs bright,
And Confessors arrayed in white,
Let us no longer exil'd roam,
But call us to our heavenly home.

5 Chaste virgins, and you truly wise,
Who from the deserts filled the skies,
For us an everlasting reign
With Christ among His saints obtain.

6 From Christian lands those faithless chase
Who Christian truths and faith deface;
That all mankind united may
One Pastor of their souls obey.

7 To God the Father, and the Son,
And Holy Spirit, Three in One,
Be equal glory, equal praise,
For an eternal age of days.

73. *All Saints' Day.*

1 Hail! feast of deep celestial joy,
   Linking earth with heaven,
Happy saints enwreathed with light,
Streaming from God's blessed sight,
   Praise to you be given.

2 Ye angel bands who ever sing,
   Songs of seraphic praise,
Saints and martyrs swelling high,
Heaven's celestial harmony,
   With yours our voice we raise.

3 Sweet Virgin Mother brighter far
   Than brightest seraph there,
Where the light of God is seen
Thou dost reign a beauteous Queen,
   The fairest of the fair.

4 Oh, for the blissful dawn to rise
   Scattering clouds of night!
When shall troubled hearts find rest,
'Mid the regions of the blest,
   'Mid homes of dear delight?

5 Ye saddened spirits, stay your fears,
   Grief will soon be o'er,
Hope e'en now with cheering ray,
Tells the dawn of brighter day,
   On heaven's eternal shore.

6 Then bravely on with joyous heart,
    Trustful with childlike love,
  Tracing the path which saints have trod
  The homeward way which leads to God,
    To blissful realms above.

VII. THE CHURCH.

74. *The Pillar of Truth.*

1 One Body, one Spirit, one Lord,
    And one Faith for all ages was given,
  One Baptism, framed to accord
    With one God, and one Father in Heaven,
  One Church,—the sole Pillar and Ground
    Of the Truth,—an immoveable Rock ;
  One Shepherd by all to be own'd,
    And one Fold for that primitive Flock !

2 One Ark in whose refuge to trust
    In the tempests that faith has to brave,
  While others are sway'd by each gust
    Of opinion, or lost in its wave.
  One House for the people of God,
    One theme for the sinner in prayer,
  One Path to the blessed abode
    Of the saints who now plead for us there.

3 That House, if the malice of hell
    Or the madness of earth could destroy,
  Had fallen and crush'd as it fell
    The belief in all truth, and its joy.

The rain fell upon it, and falls,
  And the floods came in torrents of rage;
The winds blew and beat on its walls,
  But it fell not, nor trembles from age.

---

75. *The Church.*

1 Who is she that stands triumphant,
    Rock in strength, upon the Rock,
  Like some city crowned with turrets,
    Braving storm, and earthquake shock?
  Who is she her arms extending
    In blessing o'er a world restored;
  All the anthems of creation
    Lifting to creation's Lord?

CHORUS.

Hers the kingdom, hers the sceptre!
  Kneel, ye nations, at her feet!
Hers that Truth whose fruit is Freedom; ⎫
  Light her yoke; her burthen sweet! ⎬ Repeat.

2 As the moon that takes its splendour
    From a sun unseen all night,
  So from Christ, the Sun of Justice,
    Evermore She draws her light.
  Hers alone the hands of healing,
    The Bread of Life, th' absolving Key:
  The Word Incarnate is her Bridegroom,
    The Spirit hers, His temple, she.
        Chorus.—Hers the kingdom, &c.

3 Empires rise and sink like billows;
    Their place knoweth them no more:
Glorious as the star of morning
    She o'erlooks the wild uproar.
Hers the Household all embracing;
    Hers the Vine that shadows earth:
Blest thy children, mighty mother!
    Safe the stranger at thy hearth!
        Chorus.—Hers the kingdom, &c.

76. *The Holy Roman Church.*

1 I'll never forsake thee, I never will be,
O Church of the Saints, an apostate from thee,
Though friends may entice me, and fortune
    may frown,
My Faith and my Church until death I will
    own.

2 They may boast of their wealth, they may talk
    of their gold,
I'll be true to the Faith like the Martyrs of old,
" A Catholic live, and a Catholic die,"
Be this my life's watchword, at death my last
    cry.

3 I may lose some advantage and forfeit some
    gain,
I may meet with unkindness and suffer some
    pain,
But Jesus and Mary will surely bestow
Richer gifts than from sin and apostasy flow.

4 They call me a Papist and laugh at my creed,
  'Tis the faith that will save in the hour of need;
  Let them talk, let them laugh, but when death
    is at hand,
  The priest is the only true friend in the land.

5 Then we'll cling to the Priest, and we'll cling
    to the Pope;
  We'll cling to Christ's Vicar, for Christ is our
    hope;
  We'll fight a good battle and Mary the while
  From her throne in the skies on her children
    will smile.

---

77. *England's Conversion.*

Repeat the last two lines of every verse.

1 England! Oh, what means this sighing
  From those heaps of mossy stone;
  As of spirits music trying
  On some harp, left crushed and lone?
Through carved shaft of aisles deserted,
  Breezes murmur still the song,
Which, in cadence sweet concerted
  Rais'd once there the cloister'd throng.

CHORUS.

  Holy Household of sweet Nazareth,
    Jesus, Mary, Joseph! down
  On each servant look, who gathereth
    Flowers for England's future crown;

Hill, plain, valley, garden, heath,
Yield your bloom for England's wreath!

2 Whence this clang of pick and hammer,
Blent with cheers in field and town?
Ha! whence that unearthly clamour,
'Neath earth's lowest deeps far down?
There is Faith once more restoring
Church and Convent, cross and spire:
Here perdition's host is roaring
Cries of vengeance, howls of ire.
Chorus.—Holy Household, &c.

3 Earth and Heaven's Saints are praying,
"Haste, O God! Thy gracious boon!"
We poor sinners whisper, saying,
"Jesus! save dear England soon!"
Hark! above the bells are ringing
Merry peals from shore to shore;
Higher still are Angels singing,
"England! Mary's child once more!"
Chorus.—Holy Household, &c.

78. *Faith of our Fathers.*

The words in Italics apply to Ireland, and may be substituted for the
text below when fitting.

1 Faith of our Fathers! living still,
In spite of dungeon, fire, and sword:
Oh, $\left\{\begin{array}{l}\textit{Ireland's}\\ \text{how our}\end{array}\right\}$ hearts beat high with joy

Whene'er $\left\{\begin{array}{l}\textit{they}\\ \text{we}\end{array}\right\}$ hear that glorious word;

CHORUS.

Faith of our Fathers ! Holy Faith !
We will be true to thee till death.

2 Our Fathers, chained in prisons dark,
   Were still in heart and conscience free :
How sweet would be their children's fate,
   If they, like them, could die for Thee.
          Chorus.—Faith of our Fathers, &c.

3 Faith of our Fathers ! Mary's prayers,
  { *Shall keep our country fast to thee ;* }
  { Shall win our country back to thee ; }
And through the truth that comes from God,
  { *O we shall prosper and be free.* }
  { England shall then indeed be free, }
          Chorus.—Faith of our Fathers, &c.

4 Faith of our Fathers ! we will love
   Both friend and foe in all our strife :
And preach thee too, as love knows how,
   By kindly words and virtuous life.
          Chorus.—Faith of our Fathers, &c.

VIII. THE CHRISTIAN LIFE.

79. *Young Men's Hymn.*

1 The Cross ! the Cross ! ye young men all !
Ye soldiers bound to grace's call !
A league is signed 'twixt heaven and you
In blood which shines on foreheads true,

That ev'ry sin ye'll shun and fly
Soon as its plague-spot ye descry
That pleasure ne'er with pleasing wile,
Nor pain, shall from your God beguile.

CHORUS.

Praise to Jesus' love unending,
 Praise to Him who died to save;
May His grace through life extending ⎫
 Crown us in the strife we brave ! ⎬ *Repeat.*
                                    ⎭

2 A palace bright and throne most fair,
 A crownlet deck'd with jewels rare,
 Are yours to hold and yours to win
 In fight which now you wage with sin
 The battle day will soon be o'er,
 Your Lord hath trod the field before ;
 His faith your shield, His hope your helm,
 No terror shall your souls o'erwhelm.
      Chorus.—Praise to Jesus, &c.

3 Be chaste and gentle, kind and true,
 Of word or deed have nought to rue,
 Seek Mary's favour, Mary's love,
 And live on earth with her above:
 Through her your hearts to Jesus give,
 And here in holy concord live,
 Till of your home, that's ever nigh,
 The gates unfold at death's last sigh.
      Chorus.—Praise to Jesus, &c.

80. *A Young Man's Colloquy with Jesus.*

Repeat the two last lines of each verse.

1 How sweet and pure Thy call divine
    That claims my youthful heart,
It tells me I may still be Thine
    And see Thee as Thou art:
It makes me long for joys unknown,
    And sigh to burst life's ties;
One end in life it makes me own
    And count all other—lies.

2 No more the world shall hold its sway,
    Nor vain, nor silly pride;
Religion's pure and genial ray
    Shall be my light and guide.
If one affection still remain,
    That clings not all to Thee,
Then break the bond, I heed no pain,
    So that my soul be free!

3 I give it Thee—Thou claim'st no more,
    'Though poor the offering be;
Alas! my heart is all the store
    That I can give to Thee.
Then take it Lord! 'tis all Thine own,
    It sighs! it sighs! for Thee:
Here fix for ever, Lord! Thy throne,
    Thus shall I happy be.

81. *Salvation.*

Repeat the last line of every verse.

1 Strive ye salvation to attain,
   'Tis easy to a willing mind,
To every Christian, highest gain,
   Seek then, pursue it till ye find.

CHORUS.
Repeat.

Unless salvation we obtain,
All treasures of earth are vain.

2 Salvation lost, we lose our all,
   Lose our celestial heritage,
In hell's dark depths we're doomed to fall,
   Oh! may this all our thoughts engage.
      Chorus.—Unless salvation, &c.

3 What profit for us to obtain
   The widespread mighty universe;
If doomed to never-ending pain
   In hell's fierce flames? oh! fearful curse!
      Chorus.—Unless salvation, &c.

4 Nothing is worthy our desire
   But life eternal and divine,
All else, 'tis folly to require,
   Let no such folly, then, be mine.
      Chorus.—Unless salvation, &c.

5 It is for all eternity
  That we enjoy our heavenly bliss,
Or writhe in endless misery—
  What thought so full of awe as this !
    Chorus.—Unless salvation, &c.

6 Oh! Lord ordain, while we remain
  On earth, this truth may penetrate
Our inmost souls, till we obtain
  Our blessed and immortal state.
    Chorus.—Unless salvation, &c.

---

82. *The Four Great Truths.*

1 There is one true and only God,
  Our Maker and our Lord :
And He created everything
  By His Almighty Word.

CHORUS.

All this—and all the Church doth teach,
  My God ! I do believe ;
For Thou hast bid us hear the Church,
  And Thou canst not deceive.

2 But in this One and only God
  There yet are Persons Three ;
The Father, Son, and Holy Ghost,—
  One Blessed Trinity.
    Chorus.—All this, &c.

3 The Second Person—God the Son,
    Came down on earth to dwell ;
Took flesh, and died upon the Cross,
    To save our souls from Hell.
          Chorus.—All this, &c.

4 The good, with God in heaven above
    Will ever happy be ;
The wicked, in the flames of hell
    Will burn eternally.
          Chorus.—All this, &c.

---

83. *The Ten Commandments.*

I.

I am the Lord,—and thou shalt serve
    No other gods but Me :
Religion true thou shalt observe,
    Faith, Hope, and Charity.

II.

Thou shalt not take God's Name in vain,
    Nor swear unlawfully ;
Things holy thou shalt not profane,
    Nor curse irreverently.

III.

Remember that thou Sanctify
    The holy Sabbath day ;
Work not without necessity,
    Hear holy Mass, and pray.

IV.

THY PARENTS HONOUR, serve and love,
    And cheerfully obey;
And servants must obedient prove
    When without sin they may.

V.

THOU SHALT NOT KILL—nor vengeance take,
    Nor hate thy enemy:
Forgive and love for Jesus's sake
    All that have injured thee.

The same commandment does beside,
    Forbid all drunkenness,
Self injury and suicide,
    And eating to excess.

VI.

DO NOT COMMIT ADULTERY,
    In thoughts, words, deeds or looks;
Beware of evil company,
    And read not dangerous books.

VII.

THOU SHALT NOT STEAL, nor keep, nor waste,
    Nor cheat in any way:
Ill-gotten goods restore in haste,
    And lawful debts repay.

VIII.

FALSE WITNESS THOU SHALT NEVER BEAR,
    Nor tell a wilful lie:
Detraction, if thou canst repair,
    As well as calumny.

IX and X.

THOU SHALT NOT COVET NEIGHBOUR'S WIFE,
  Nor look with lustful eye ;
THOU SHALT NOT COVET NEIGHBOUR'S GOODS,
  Nor eye them enviously.

All this Thou dost command, O Lord !
  We cheerfully obey ;
And look to heaven for our reward
  Through all eternity.

---

84. *The Seven Sacraments.*

1 The Church has SEVEN SACRAMENTS,
  As we must all believe :
But THREE there are more requisite
  To know and to receive.

2 BAPTISM washes out the sin
  Which Adam did commit :
The sins which we ourselves have done,
  CONFESSION will remit.

3 The EUCHARIST we know to be
  The Body and Blood divine
Of Jesus Christ, both God and man,
  In form of bread and wine.

4 In CONFIRMATION we believe
  The Holy Ghost is given :
· In EXTREME UNCTION we get strength
  To die and go to Heaven.

5 By Holy Orders, priests are made,
    And get both Power and Grace :
And Matrimony blesses those
    Who married life embrace.

6 All praise and thanks to Jesus be,
    And to His Holy Blood,
By which we have the Sacraments,
    The source of every good.

————

85. *I nothing fear with Jesus at my side.*

1 To win my heart with visions bright and fair,
    In vain the world with all its craft has tried :
Harmless and weak its dazzling weapons are
    I nothing fear, with Jesus at my side. } Repeat.
    Repeat.

2 Come all ye proud ones of the earth, array
    Your gathering hosts around me far and wide ;
My heart is calm amid the loud affray,
    I nothing fear with Jesus at my side. (*as above.*)

3 Lift up thy banner, armed in all thy rage,
    With all thy followers, thou prince of pride ;
Though single here I stand this war to wage ;
    I nothing fear with Jesus at my side. (*as above.*)

4 Death has for me no fears, its bitter pains
    Shall never from my King my heart divide :
Faithful to death, to Him my will remains ;
    I nothing fear with Jesus at my side. (*as above.*)

5 Though all the terrors of the last dread day,
  With earth and hell together were allied :
  Though heaven and earth before me fled away,
  I nothing fear with Jesus at my side. (*as above.*)

6 Jesus my Lord ! my only hope and shield ;
  No powers of ill before Thee can abide ;
  My trust in Thee upon the battle field,
  I nothing fear with Jesus at my side. (*as above.*)

------

86. *The Vanity of the World.*

1   All things on earth are vain,
     Short-lived, and full of pain,
  Though hidden in apparent glee,
  By the vain world proposed to me,
     All this brilliant display !
       This vain show !
     The pride of a day !
       All must go :
  It fades from the sight,
  For oh ! 'tis as fleeting as bright.

2   As do the fairest flowers,
     We've watched through summer hours,
  In their prime but bloom and die ;
  And their beauty is gone for aye :
     So is it with beauty's charms,
       Sure the lot !
     Amidst life's alarms,
       Is it not?
  With her who was queen,
  A blight ! and she is no more seen.

3   His happiness to gain,
 Erring youth seeks to drain
Of luxury the poison'd bowl,
In the hand of the tempter fell:
 But the more he goes astray,
  Wretched and lone!
 The sport of a day!
  He's borne on,
 To bitter remorse,
In sure and unchangeable course.

4   Then in the midst of pride,
 Life's treasures opened wide,
And with many to call him blest,
With many to do his behest:
 All is emptiness and grief!
  When alone!
 E'en scorn were relief!
  To atone,
And lighten sin's doom,
Whilst penance for merit finds room.

5   Foolish then is the man,
 Who in earth's little span,
Will vainly set his hopes of rest;
And for God take the world unblest!
 For the Lord of Life,—'tis known,
  No surprise,—
 As in all time shown,
  Will arise,
With judgments diverse,
The heralds of blessing and curse.

87. *Fight for Sion.*

CHORUS.

Christians! to the war!
Gather from afar!
Hark! hark! the word is given;
Jesus bids us fight
" For God and the right,"
And for Mary, the Queen of Heaven!

1 Now first for thee, thou wicked world!
  Puffed up with godless pomp and pageant,
Avenging grace to humble thee
  Can make the weakest arm its agent.
    Chorus.—Christians! to the war! &c.

2 And thou, dark fiend, six thousand years
  The bride of Christ in vain tormenting,
Shall find our hate and scorn of thee
  Deep as thine own, and unrelenting.
    Chorus.—Christians! to the war! &c.

3 Ah Self! so oft forgiven, thou
  Canst play no part but that of traitor;
We spare thy life but thou must bear
  The felon's brand, the captive's fetter.
    Chorus.—Christians! to the war! &c.

4 But worse than devil, flesh, or world,
  Human respect, like poison creeping,
Chills and unnerves the hosts of Christ,
  When weary war-worn hearts are sleeping.
    Chorus.—Christians! to the war! &c.

5 Like lions roaring for their prey,
    Armies of foes are round us trooping;
What then? see countless angels come
    To heal the hurt, to raise the drooping.
        Chorus. —Christians! to the war! &c.

6 Then bravely, comrades to the fight,
    With shout and song each other cheering;
Strength not our own from heaven descends,
    The sun breaks out, the clouds are clearing.
        Chorus.—Christians! to the war! &c.

7 On, to the gates of Sion, on!
    Break through the foe with fresh endeavour;
We'll hang our colours up in heaven,
    When peace shall be proclaimed for ever.
        Chorus.- —Christians! to the war! &c.

———

88. *The Christian Soldier.*

1 Oh! God of armies, hear our vow,
    And make our purpose strong,
We vow to fight for Thee till death,
    Our hearts to Thee belong:
We'll never yield our souls to sin,
    Nor do the tempter's will,
We'd rather die and forfeit all,
    If we may love Thee still.

CHORUS.

Then Warriors on, come battle for the Lord,
Resolved to fight, and never sheathe the sword
Till God shall call us to our home above
And fill us with perpetual peace and love. } Repeat.

2 We know how weak and frail we are,
    We mourn our former sins,
Be Thou our strength, we trust in Thee,
    Thy grace it is that wins :
Beneath Thy banner we will fight,
    Our banner, hope shall be,
Faith is our shield, and love our sword,
    With these we'll come to Thee.
      Chorus.—Then warriors on, &c.

3 We'll come to Thee, whoe'er withstands,
    We'll come in spite of all ;
We'll trample on the world and flesh,
    The demons too shall fall :
For Thou art God, the Strong in war,
    And we Thy warriors be,
Never shall sin usurp this earth,
    This earth belongs to Thee.
      Chorus.—Then warriors on, &c.

---

89. *The Christian's Song on his March to Heaven.*

1 Blest is the Faith, divine and strong,
    Of thanks and praise an endless fountain,
Whose life is one perpetual song,
    High up the Saviour's holy mountain.

CHORUS.

O Sion's songs are sweet to sing
  With melodies of gladness laden ;
Hark ! how the harps of angels ring,
  Hail, Son of Man ! Hail, Mother-Maiden !
                              [Repeat the last line.

2 Blest is the hope that holds to God,
    In doubt and darkness still unshaken,
  And sings along the heavenly road
    Sweetest when most it seems forsaken.
      Chorus.—O Sion's songs, &c.

3 Blest is the love that cannot love
    Aught that earth gives of best and brightest;
  Whose raptures thrill, like saints above,
    Most when its earthly gifts are lightest.
      Chorus.—O Sion's songs, &c.

4 Blest is the death that good men die,
    Solemn, self-doubting, firm and wary,
  Trusting to God its destiny
    And leaning for its hour on Mary.
      Chorus.—O Sion's songs, &c.

90. *The Pilgrims of the Night.*

1 Hark! hark ! my soul! angelic songs are swelling
    O'er earth's green fields, and ocean's wave-
        beat shore !
  How sweet the truth, those blessed strains are
      telling,
    Of that new life when sin shall be no more !

CHORUS.

Angels of Jesus!
Angels of light!
Singing to welcome
The pilgrims of the night. } *Repeat.*

2 Darker than night life's shadows fall around us,
And, like benighted men, we miss our mark;
God hides Himself, and grace hath scarcely
found us,
Ere death finds out his victims in the dark.
Chorus.—Angels of Jesus, &c.

3 Onward we go, for still we hear them singing,
Come weary souls! for Jesus bids you come!
And through the dark, its echoes sweetly ring-
ing,
The music of the gospel leads us home.
Chorus.—Angels of Jesus! &c.

4 Far, far away, like bells at evening pealing,
The voice of Jesus sounds o'er land and sea,
And laden souls, by thousands meekly stealing,
Kind Shepherd! turn their weary steps to
Thee.
Chorus.—Angels of Jesus, &c.

5 Rest comes at length, though life be long and
dreary,
The day must dawn, and darksome night be
past;

All journeys end in welcomes to the weary,
    And heaven, the heart's true home, will come
      at last.
        Chorus.—Angels of Jesus, &c.

6 Cheer up my soul! faith's moonbeams softly
      glisten
    Upon the breast of life's most troubled sea;
And it will cheer thy drooping heart to listen
    To those brave songs which angels mean for
      thee.
        Chorus.—Angels of Jesus, &c.

7 Angels! sing on, your faithful watches keep-
      ing,
    Sing us sweet fragments of the songs above,
While we toil on, and soothe ourselves with
      weeping,
    Till life's long night shall break in endless
      love.

CHORUS.

Angels of Jesus!
  Angels of light!
Singing to welcome
  The darkness of the night.

----

91. *The Wounded Heart.*

1 The wounded heart loves on and weeps,
    And never doubts its Father's care:
But softly to the cross it creeps,
    And finds its watchful Mother there.

It never doubts in cold dismay,
    Nor turns rebellious 'neath the rod,
But evermore, by night and day,
    Knows that its sorrows come from God.

2 For every pain is meted out,
    And every sorrow knows its place ;
It bears them all without a doubt,
    And looks up in its Father's face.
And then it knows how He has given ;
    Two hearts to help it in the strife ;
The two Immaculate of Heaven,
    Who led the deepest suffering life.

3 So to the cross it gently creeps,
    For hope shines ever brightly there,
And as it goes, it loves and weeps,
    To think how they its sorrows share.
And God is felt in all His power,
    Serenely calm and sweetly still ;
The faithful heart in sorrow's hour,
    Bows in submission to His will.

---

92. *For a Happy Death.*

1 Jesus ! ever loving Saviour
    Thou didst live and die for me ;
Living, I will live to love Thee,
    Dying, I will die for Thee.
      Jesus ! Jesus !
By Thy life and death of sorrow,
    Help me in my agony.

2 When the last dread hour approaching
   Fills my guilty soul with fear,
All my sins rise up before me,
   All my virtues disappear.
       Jesus! Jesus!
Turn not Thou in anger from me;
   Mary! Joseph! then be near.

3 Kindest Jesus! Thou wert standing
   By Thy foster-father's bed,
While Thy mother softly praying,
   Held her dying Joseph's head.
       Jesus! Jesus!
By that death so calm and holy,
   Soothe me in that hour of dread.

4 Mary! Thou canst not forsake me,
   Virgin Mother undefiled!
Thou didst not abandon Jesus,
   Dying tortured and reviled.
       Jesus! Jesus!
Send Thy Mother to console me;
   Mary! help thy guilty child.

5 Jesus! when in cruel anguish
   Dying on the shameful tree,
All abandon'd by Thy Father,
   Thou didst writhe in agony.
       Jesus! Jesus!
By those three long hours of sorrow,
   Thou didst purchase hope for me.

6 When the priest with holy unction
   Prays for mercy and for grace,
 May the tears of deep compunction
   All my guilty stains efface.
       Jesus! Jesus!
 Let me find in Thee a refuge,
   In Thy heart a resting-place.

7 If my eyes have sinn'd by seeing,
   And my hands are stain'd with blood,
 If I sinn'd by taste or hearing,
   If my feet in vice have stood;
       Jesus! Jesus!
 Thy most pure and guiltless senses,
   All have suffer'd for my good.

8 Then by all that Thou didst suffer,
   Grant me mercy in that day!
 Help me, Mary, my sweet Mother!
   Holy Joseph, near me stay!
       Jesus! Jesus!
 Let me die, my lips repeating,
   Jesus mercy! Mary pray!

IX. MISSIONS AND RETREATS.

93. *Hail, Holy Mission, Hail!*

1 Hail, holy Mission, hail!
   Sighing we turn to thee,
 For weary have we found
   The path of sin to be.

2 Hail, holy Mission, hail !
　　Sent to us from above ;
When Jesus with His cross
　　Comes to win back our love.

3 Hail, holy Mission, hail !
　　Time of repentant tears ;
When to the soul returns
　　The peace of former years.

4 Hail, holy Mission, hail !
　　Sweet time of humble prayer ;
When rests the soul on God.
　　Freed from this dark world's care.

5 Hail, holy Mission, hail !
　　Time of all others blest ;
When in the loving soul,
　　Jesus takes up His rest.

6 Hail, holy Mission, hail !
　　Foretaste of joys above ;
O ! Jesus, make our hearts
　　Burn with Thy tender love.

94.　*On Death.*

CHORUS.

On to death, on to death
　　We are hurrying fast :
This hour, nay this moment
　　May be the last.

1 We all must die, our doom is fixed,
　　Nor youth, nor strength, nor art can save,
　As sure as now we tread the earth,
　　So sure we're hastening to the grave.
　　　Chorus.—On to death, &c.

2 For He has spoke that mighty word
　　Whose bidding none can e'er withstand,
　As pilgrims we're upon this earth
　　Who journey towards a better land.
　　　Chorus.—On to death, &c.

3 Then think, my soul! the day is near,
　　When thou upon thy bed shalt lie,
　And thy pale face and shrivell'd form
　　Shall warn thy friends that death is nigh.
　　　Chorus.—On to death, &c.

4 When gathering round thy couch they'll stand,
　　And sadly gaze upon thy face,
　Will whisper low, but still their looks
　　Will plainly show that death they trace.
　　　Chorus.—On to death, &c.

5 Farewell, farewell to all thou leavest,
　　Thy wife, thy children, riches, friends;
　The world may smile while life endures,
　　But all is gone before it ends!
　　　Chorus.—On to death, &c.

6 Then bid at once farewell to sin,
　　Nor leave thy guilty deeds behind,
　In loathsome grasp to hold thee fast,
　　The bitter taste of sin to find.
　　　Chorus.—On to death, &c.

7 The clock has struck the fatal hour,
    The wearied heart has ceased to beat,
The eyes are vacant, glassy, dead,
    And motionless the hands and feet.
        Chorus.—On to death, &c.

8 But where, oh! where, now stands the soul?
    It stands before God's awful throne,
Without a friend to plead its cause
    Before its God it stands alone.
        Chorus.—On to death, &c.

95.   *The Sinner conscience-stricken.*

1   Alas!
    What grief and care
    My heart-strings tear,
  And tears my cheeks bedew!
      Alas!
    What grief and care
    My heart-strings tear,
 With dread well-nigh despair—
        'Twas not so
  When Thy ways were new;
        Oh Lord, no!
  For I call'd Thee true—
      Alas!
    Vows made in vain!
    Days full of pain!
  Can peace be mine again?

2   There's death
Almost in sight,
With his sad night
From which in fear I shrink:
  There's death
Almost in sight
With his sad night
To rob me for aye of light:
   Yes I fear
Death makes now my bed;
   Well I hear
His stern voice so dread—
    O tomb!
O cruel tomb!
Dark house of gloom,
In youth how hard my doom.

3   Behold
The penance dire
In wrathful fire
Which none may call severe:
  Behold
The penance dire
In wrathful fire
The proof of God's just ire.
   'Tis sin's cost
Those fires, I fear,
   If I'm lost!
Hell, how shall I bear!
    I'll turn
To God to-day
My doom to stay
And mend without delay.

4   Ah, me !
What sounds of fear
Assault my ear,
What flames dark shadows cast :
Ah me !
What sounds of fear
Assault my ear
From trumpet echoes clear.
Haste away !
Mercy's hour is past !
No delay !
Vengeance comes at last.
O God !
'Tis hell I see :—
And, hating Thee,
The damned in agony.

5   O Heav'n
And art thou lost
With all thou'st cost,
Sold for a shameful treat—
O heav'n
And art thou lost
With all thou'st cost,
To leave remorse's frost—
Lost to thee,—
Thy pleasures most sweet
Bring to me,
Retribution meet—
O heav'n
My hope before
My God t' adore !
To thee I look no more.

6   O ye
Friends of my youth,
Strong in God's truth,
In heav'n ye now rejoice—
    O ye
Friends of my youth,
Strong in God's truth,
To me there is no ruth—
    To my cost,
Vain wisdom I sought:
    And I lost,
The virtue you wrought.
    Yes ye
In heaven dwell,
Who sin repel,
For me there's nought but hell.

7   Oh no!
It can't be so
For in my woe
True love I put to shame,
    Oh no!
It is not so
For in my woe
My Jesus I forego—
    I'll arise
His mercy to claim,
    And I'll prize
Grace, through His sweet name.
    His name!—
Yes, through His name
Contrition's flame
Has made Him mine again.

8   Jesus !
          My only rest
          Food of the blest
      In grief my sins I trace.
             Jesus !
          My only rest
          Food of the blest
      Receive me as Thy guest.
             Joy restore !
          Sin pardon'd efface,
             Evermore
          By virtue of grace.
             Jesus !
          Be Thou ador'd
          The sinner's Lord,
      By love his hope reward.

---

96.   *God and the Sinner.*

Repeat the last line of each verse.

GOD.

1 O Sinner come unto thy God—nor later
    Delay to bend to God thy rebel knee ;
Against His law too long thou'st been a traitor,
    Return to Him since He returns to thee.

SINNER.

2 Behold O Lord ! this lost and straying sheep
    Whom Thou didst deign to seek for, oh !
        how long !
Aroused at last from its long deadly sleep,
    Guilty, confus'd, this heart repents its wrong.

GOD.

3 To call thee back My voice has long resounded,
  I've followed thee with blessings far and near;
Wounding thy God's—a Father's heart thou'st
    wounded,
Ungrateful still wilt thou refuse to hear?

SINNER.

4 Ah dearest Lord! I sought, but sought in vain
  A spot where I might lose the dread of Thee,
Wand'ring and lost, how could I know but pain,
  Estrang'd from Thee—and Thou estrang'd
    from me.

GOD.

5 Now grief, now joy; now terror and remorse,
  In tender love I sent thee o'er and o'er,
With grace I tried to stay thy headlong course,
  My grace was spurned—but still I offer more.

SINNER.

6 Yea, Lord! I do repent me sore and sadly,
  Yea, Father! tho' I've sinn'd 'gainst Thee
    and heav'n,
Forgive, forget the course I've run so madly,
  And breathe the blessed words, "Thou art
    forgiven."

GOD.

7 Repentant son thy heart is all I seek,
  And when thy heart is given all to Me,
My mercy takes thy service, render'd meek,
  And rains down grace and love unceasingly.

SINNER.

8 My God! how good Thou art to all Thy sons,
Who with sincerity their sins deplore—
With grief and love my swelling heart o'er-runs,
Oh give me grace to love Thee evermore.

---

97. *The Wages of Sin.*

1 O what are the wages of sin,
The end of the race we have run?
We have slaved for the master we chose,
And what is the prize we have won?

CHORUS.

Wo are worn out and weary with sin;
Its pleasures are poor at the best;
From what we remember, not worth
Half an hour of a conscience at rest.

2 We gave away all things for sin,—
And oh! it was much that was given,—
The love of the angels and saints,
And the chance of our getting to heaven.
Chorus.—We are worn out, &c.

3 We gave away Jesus and God,
We gave away Mary and grace,
Prayer and Confession and Mass;
And now we have finished the race!
Chorus.—We are worn out, &c.

4 For sin in the hand, is not like
  The bright thing it looked to the eye;
  Its taste is still worse than its touch;
  Yet we swallow the poison and die.
            Chorus.—We are worn out, &c.

5 O fools that we were! can we now
  Break off the bad bargain we made?
  And is there a way to get back
  The precious deposit we paid?
            Chorus.—We are worn out, &c.

6 O yes, we have got but to send
  One word or one sigh up to heaven;
  The mischief will be all undone,
  And the past completely forgiven.
            Chorus.—We are worn out, &c.

7 Jesus is just what He was,
  On the cross, as we left Him before,
  All gentleness, mercy, and love,
  Nay, His love and His mercy look more.
            Chorus.—We are worn out, &c.

8 We will back with our hearts in our hands—
  For the heart is His regular fee;
  Forgive us, dear Jesus, forgive—
  All we want is forgiveness and Thee.
            Chorus.—We are worn out, &c.

---

98. *Hymn of Repentant Sorrow.*

1 Jesus, my God, behold at length the time,
  When I resolve to turn away from crime,

O Pardon me, Jesus, Thy mercy I implore,
I will never more offend Thee, no, never more.

2 Since my poor soul Thy precious blood hath cost,
Suffer me not for ever to be lost !
         Chorus.—O pardon me, &c.

3 Behold me then, Jesus, behold me at Thy feet,
Like Mary in tears, forgiveness I entreat.
         Chorus.—O pardon me, &c.

99. *Act of Contrition.*

1 God of mercy and compassion !
    Look with pity upon me !
Father! let me call Thee Father !
    ' Tis Thy child returns to Thee !

Jesus! Lord! I ask for mercy,
    Let me not implore in vain !
All my sins—I now detest them,
    Never will I sin again.

2 By my sins I have deserved
    Death and endless misery ;
Hell, with all its pains and torments,
    And for all eternity !
         Chorus.—Jesus! Lord! &c.

3 By my sins I have abandoned
   Right and claim to heaven above;
Where the Saints rejoice for ever
   In a boundless sea of Love.
         Chorus.—Jesus! Lord! &c.

4 See our Saviour, bleeding, dying,
   On the Cross of Calvary,
To that Cross my sins have nailed Him,
   Yet He bleeds and dies for me.
         Chorus.—Jesus! Lord! &c.

----

100. *The Triumphs of Grace.*

Repeat the last line of each verse.

1 Joy, joy to the choir celestial
When a soul is restored to grace,
God owns a new throne terrestrial
When weak man in truth seeks His face—
Joy, joy to the pardon'd sinner,
Whom God in His mercy hath blest;
With His love, above all other
And the promise of endless rest.

CHORUS.

    Singing praise to our God,
    Singing praise to His grace,
We'll seek, we'll seek, the path His Saints trod,
We'll seek, we'll seek, His will to embrace.

2 Thrice blest is the state of grace,
For 'tis peace and joy to the mind,
And hope, that can sorrow efface
Teaching patience of every kind—

Then God's grace alone we will prize,
As our life and our heavenly light;
For who but the fool would despise
The gift of love's infinite might?

CHORUS.

Singing praise to our God,
Singing praise to His grace,
We'll love, we'll love, the path His saints trod,
We'll love, we'll love, His will to embrace.

3 Blessed too, the prize grace ensures
When the end of our work is shown,
The reward to love that endures
In the glory of Heav'n is known—
For then Jesus will crown His own
With a crown unspeakably bright,
Which He gives to His brethren alone,
Who have stood with Him in the fight.

CHORUS.

Singing praise to our God,
Singing praise to His grace,
We'll run, we'll run, the path His saints trod,
We'll run, we'll run, His will to embrace.

X. THE HEREAFTER.

101. *Purgatory.*

1 Buried deep in flames we lie,
Patiently we weep and sigh,
Far from God we wait in pain
Till our souls are pure again.

Alas! Alas!

All the tears which we can shed
Cannot quench our fiery bed.

2 Seeing thus the pains we bear,
Christians hear us, grant our prayer;
Have compassion on our woe,
Take us hence, we long to go.
Alas! Alas!
God is just,—unless you pray
We must weep and pine away.

3 You can save us from our pangs,
From this fire's piercing fangs;
Quickly save us, Brothers kind!
God will hear with ready mind.
Alas! Alas!
When shall we escape these flames?
Are we still defiled with stains?

4 God of justice, Mary pleads,
And Thy mercy intercedes;
Cause our sorrow now to cease,
Let Christ's Blood be our release.
Alas! Alas!
Are Thy liberating Hands
Still unmoved to loose our bands?

---

102. Heaven.

1 Oh Heaven! celestial home!·
    Oh boundless land of love,
  I long to enter thee
    And see my God above.

When will the angels come
And call my soul away?
This earth is dark as night,
But heaven is bright as day.

2 Why stay I here so long,
An exile from the land
Where Mary sits enthron'd
Upon her Son's right hand?
Chorus. —When will, &c.

3 Pleading with tenderest love,
For all who breathe the name
Of Him who was, who is,
And e'er will be the same.
Chorus.—When will, &c.

4 Jesus Thy love is more
Than mortal tongue can sing,
The fountain of my Faith,
My hope, my ev'rything.
Chorus.—When will, &c.

5 If death no terror brings,
'Tis lasting, burning love
That fills my soul with zeal
To reach my God above.
Chorus.—When will, &c.

6 Sad sighs and tears, my lot
'Till th' angel's trumpet sounds,
To bid me glorious rise
To lands where joy abounds.
Chorus.—When will, &c.

7 Before the throne divine,
  My voice at length I'll raise,
To God in Persons three,
  With Hymns of endless praise.
        Chorus.—When will, &c.

---

103. "*Heaven is the prize.*"

1 Yes, Heaven is the prize
  My soul shall strive to gain,
One glimpse of paradise
  Repays a life of pain.

CHORUS.

Tis Heaven!—'tis Heaven!—yes, Heaven is
the prize!

2 Yes, Heaven is the prize!
  My soul, oh think of this!
All earthly goods despise,
  For such a crown of bliss.
        Chorus.—'Tis Heaven, &c.

3 Yes, Heaven is the prize!
  When sorrows press around,
Look up beyond the skies
  Where hope and strength are found.
        Chorus.—'Tis Heaven, &c.

4 Yes, Heaven is the prize!
  Oh, 'tis not hard to gain,
He surely wins who tries;—
  For hope can conquer pain.
        Chorus.—'Tis Heaven, &c.

5 Yes, Heaven is the prize!
  The strife will soon be past.
Faint not! but raise your eyes
  And struggle to the last.
            Chorus.—'Tis Heaven, &c.

6 Yes, Heaven is the prize!
  Faith shows the crown to gain,—
Hope lights the way, and dies—
  But Love will always reign.
            Chorus.—'Tis Heaven, &c.

7 Yes, Heaven is the prize!
  Too much cannot be given,
And he alone is wise
  Who gives up all for Heaven.
            Chorus.—'Tis Heaven, &c.

8 Yes, Heaven is the prize!
  Death opens wide the door,
And then the spirit flies
  To God for evermore.
            Chorus.—'Tis Heaven, &c.

CONCLUSION.

104. *Christ's Soldiers Rise.*

1 Christ's soldier rise,
 Stand up and fight,
 In Mary's name,
 In Mary's sight.

CHORUS.

Come, take your stand,
 The world is strong,
 The foe at hand,
 The battle long.

2 Yes, we have need
 Of sword and shield ;
 The world is one
 Great battle field.
 Chorus.—Come, &c.

3 What sword shall scare
 The hostile camp ?
 A medal blest,
 With Mary's stamp.
 Chorus.—Come, &c.

4 What shield shall guard
 Christ's soldier's breast ?
 The cross that on
 His heart shall rest.
 Chorus.—Come, &c.

5 See we have foes
 Without within ;
 The devil tempts
 To mortal sin.
 Chorus.—Come, &c.

6 The devil tempts,
 But Mary's eyes
 Are on us now,
 And Satan flies.
 Chorus.—Come, &c.

7 See, Mary waves
 Her spotless flag,
 What coward in
 The rear would lag?
 Chorus.—Come, &c.

8 One shout, one prayer,
 One effort more,
 The day is ours,
 Life's struggle o'er.

CHORUS.

Come, take your crown,
 The world's undone,
 The foes are fled,
 The battle won.

105. *Veni Creator.*

1 Veni, Creátor Spíritus,
Mentes tuórum vísita,
Imple supérna grátia
Quæ tu creásti péctora.

2 Qui díceris Paráclitus,
Altíssimi donum Dei,
Fons vivus, ignis, cháritas,
Et spiritális unctio.

3 Tu septifórmis múnere
Digitus Patérnæ déxteræ,
Tu rite promíssum Pátris,
Sermóne ditans gúttura.

4 Accénde lumen sénsibus,
Infúnde amórem córdibus,
Infírma nostri córporis
Virtúte firmans pérpeti.

5 Hostem repéllas lóngius,
Pacémque dones prótinus;
Ductóre sic te prævio
Vitémus omne nóxium.

Per te sciámus da Patrem,
Noscámus atque Filium,
Teque utriúsque Spíritum
Credímus omni témpore.

106. *Come, O Creator, Spirit.*

1 Come, O Creator, Spirit blest!
And in our souls take up Thy rest;
Come, with Thy grace and heavenly aid,
To fill the hearts which Thou hast made.

2 Great Paraclete! to Thee we cry;
O highest gift of God most high!
O fount of life! O fire of love!
And sweet anointing from above.

3 Thou in Thy sevenfold gifts art known;
Thee, finger of God's hand, we own;
The promise of the Father Thou!
Who dost the tongue with power endow.

4 Our minds enlighten from above,
And make our hearts o'erflow with love;
With might of Heaven-born energy,
The weakness of our flesh supply.

5 Cast far our deadly foe away,
And grant us Thy true peace, we pray;
So shall we not, with Thee for guide,
Turn from the path of life aside.

6 Oh, may Thy grace on us bestow,
The Father and the Son to know,
And Thee through endless times confess'd
Of Both th' eternal Spirit blest.

7 Deo Pátri sit glória,
Et Fílio, qui a mórtuis
Surrexit, ac Paraclito,
In sæculórum sæcula.   Amen.

---

107. *Veni, Sancte Spiritus.*

1 Veni, Sancte Spíritus,
Et emítte cœlitus
Lucis tuæ rádium.

2 Veni, Pater paúperum,
Veni, dator múnerum,
Veni, lumen córdium.

3 Consolátor óptime,
Dulcis hospes ánimæ,
Dulce refrigérium.

4 In labóre réquies
In æstu tempéries,
In fletu solátium.

5 O lux beatíssima,
Reple cordis íntima
Tuórum fidélium.

6 Sine tuo númine,
Nihil est in hómine,
Nihil est innóxium.

7 Lava quod est sórdidum,
Riga quod est áridum,
Sana quod est sáucium.

8 Flecte quod est rígidum,
Fove quod est frígidum
Rege quod est dévium.

7 All glory while the ages run
Be to the Father, and the Son
Who rose from death ; the same to Thee,
O Holy Ghost, eternally.

---

108. *Holy Spirit ! Lord of Light.*

1 Holy Spirit ! Lord of Light !
From the clear celestial height
Thy pure beaming radiance give.

2 Come, Thou Father of the poor !
Come with treasures which endure !
Come Thou light of all that live !

3 Thou of all consolers best,
Visiting the troubled breast,
Dost refreshing peace bestow ;

4 Thou in toil art comfort sweet ;
Pleasant coolness in the heat ;
Solace in the midst of woe.

5 Light immortal ! Light divine !
Visit Thou these hearts of Thine,
And our inmost being fill :

6 If Thou take Thy grace away,
Nothing pure in man will stay
All his good is turn'd to ill.

7 Heal our wounds—our strength renew,
On our dryness pour Thy dew ;
Wash the stains of guilt away :

8 Bend the stubborn heart and will ;
Melt the frozen, warm the chill ;
Guide the steps that go astray,

10

9 Da tuis fidélibus
   In te confidéntibus,
   Sacrum septenárium.

10 Da virtútis méritum,
   Da salútis éxitum
   Da perénne gaúdium.
                  Amen.   Allelúia.

---

109.   *Adeste fideles.*

1   Adeste, fidéles,
         Læti triumphántes ;
   Veníte, veníte in Bethlehem ;
         Nátum vidéte
         Regem angelórum ;
         Veníte adorémus,
         Veníte adorémus,
   Veníte adorémus Dominum.

2   Deum de Deo,
         Lúmen de Lúmine,
   Gestant puellæ viscera :
         Deum vérum,
         Genitum non fáctum :
         Veníte adorémus, &c.

3   Cantet nunc Io
         Chorus Angelórum :
   Cantet nunc aula cœléstium,
         Gloria in excelsis Deo :
         Veníte adorémus, &c.

9 Thou on those who evermore
  Thee confess and Thee adore,
    In Thy sevenfold gifts descend :

10 Give them comfort when they die ;
   Give them life with Thee on high ;
     Give them joys which never end.

----

110. *Ye faithful, approach ye.*

1   Ye faithful, approach ye
    Joyfully triumphing ;
O come ye, O come ye, to Bethlehem ;
    Come and behold ye
    Born the King of Angels :
    O come, let us worship,
    O come, let us worship,
O come, let us worship Christ the Lord.

2   God of God,
    Light of Light,
Lo, He abhors not the Virgin's womb:
    Very God,
    Begotten, not created :
    O come let us worship, &c.

3   Sing, quires Angelic,
    Io sing exulting,
Sing, all ye citizens of Heav'n above,
    Glory to God in the highest :
    O come, let us worship, &c.

4   Ergo qui nátus
Die hodiérna,
Jesu, Tibi sit glória:
Patris æterni
Verbum caro factum:
Veníte adorémus, &c.

---

111. *Adoremus.*

Adorémus in ætérnum, sanctíssimum Sácramentum.

Laudáte Dóminum omnes gentes: laudáte eum omnes pópuli:

Quóniam confirmáta est super nos misericórdia ejus: et véritas Dómini manet in ætérnum.

Gloria Patri, &c.

---

113. *Ave Verum.*

Ave Verum Corpus, nátum
Ex María vírgine,
Vere passum, immolátum,
In cruce pro hómine.

Cujus latus perforátum
Vero fluxit sánguine.
Esto nóbis præ gustátum,
Mortis in exámine.

O clémens, O píe,
O dúlcis Jesu, Fili Mariæ.

4   Yea, Lord, we greet Thee
Born this happy morning:
Jesu, to Thee be glory given:
Word of the Father
Late in flesh appearing:
O come, let us worship, &c.

---

112. *Praise unending.*

Praise unending be to the most holy Sacrament.

Praise the LORD all ye nations: praise Him all ye people.

For His mercy is confirmed upon us: and the truth of the Lord remaineth for ever.

Glory be to the Father, &c.

---

114. *Hail to Thee.*

Hail to Thee true body sprung
From the Virgin Mary's womb!
The same that on the cross was hung
And bore for man the bitter doom!

Thou whose side was pierc'd and flow'd
Both with water and with blood;
Suffer us to taste of Thee,
In our life's last agony.

O kind! O loving One!
O sweet Jesu! Mary's Son!

115. *Adore Te devote.*

1 Adoro Te devóte, látens Deitas,
  Quæ sub his figúris vere látitas ;
  Tibi se cor meum totum súbjicit
  Quia Te contemplans totum déficit.

2 Visus gustus, tactus, in Te fallitur,
  Sed audítu solo tuto creditur.
  Credo quídquid dixit Dei Filius
  Nil hoc verbo veritátis verius.

3 In cruce latébat sóla Deitas,
  At hic latet simul et Humánitas :
  Ambo tamen credens atque confitens,
  Peto quod petívit latro pœnitens.

4 Plagas, sicut Thomas, non intueor,
  Deum tamen meum Te confíteor.
  Fac me Tibi semper magis credere,
  In Te spem habere, Te dilígere,

5 O memoriále mortis Domini !
  Panis vivus, vitam præstans homini !
  Præsta meæ menti de Te vivere,
  Et Te illi semper dulce sápere.

6 Pie Pelicáne, Jesu Domine,
  Me immundum munda Tuo sanguine,
  Cujus una stilla salvum facere,
  Totum mundum quit ab omni scelere

116. *O Godhead hid.*

Repeat the last line of every verse.

1 O Godhead hid, devoutly I adore Thee,
Who truly art within the form before me ;
To Thee my heart I bow with bended knee,
As failing quite in contemplating Thee.

2 Sight, touch, and taste, in Thee are each
deceiv'd ;
The ear alone most safely is believ'd :
I believe all the Son of God has spoken,
Than Truth's Own Word there is no truer token.

3 God only on the cross lay hid from view :
But here lies hid at once the Manhood too :
And I, in both professing my belief,
Make the same prayer as the repentant thief.

4 Thy wounds, as Thomas saw, I do not see ;
Yet Thee confess my Lord and God to be :
Make me believe Thee ever more and more ;
In Thee my hope, in Thee my love to store.

5 O Thou memorial of our Lord's own dying ;
O Bread that living art and vivifying !
Make Thou my soul henceforth on Thee to live,
Ever a taste of heavenly sweetness give.

6 O Loving Pelican ! O Jesu Lord !
Unclean I am, but cleanse me in Thy blood ;
Of which sufficient were one drop alone,
For the whole world's transgressions to atone.

7 Jesu, quem velátum nunc aspicio
　Oro, fiat illud, quod tam sitio,
　Ut, Te reveláta cernens facie,
　Visu sim beátus Tuæ gloriæ.

The following Chorus is sometimes sung after each stanza.

Ave Jesu, Pastor fidélium ;
Adauge fidem omnium in Te credentium.

––––––

117　*Lauda Sion.*

1 Lauda Sion, Salvatórem,
　　Lauda Ducem et Pastórem,
　　　In hymnis et cánticis.

2 Quantum potes, tantum aude ;
　　Quia major omni laude
　　　Nec laudáre súfficis.

3 Laudis thema speciális,
　　Panis vivus et vitális,
　　　Hódie propónitur.

4 Quem in sacræ mensa cœnæ,
　　Turbæ fratrum duodénæ
　　　Datum non ambígitur.

5 Sit laus plena, sit sonóra ;
　　Sit jucunda, sit decóra,
　　　Mentis jubilátio.

7 Jesu! whom for the present veiled I see,
What I so thirst for, oh, vouchsafe to me:
That I may see Thy countenance unfolding,
And may be blest Thy glory in beholding.

The following Chorus is sometimes sung after each stanza.

Jesu, eternal Shepherd! hear our cry;
Increase the faith of all whose souls on Thee
rely.

---

118. *Praise high thy Saviour, Sion.*

1 Praise high thy Saviour, Sion, praise
With hymns of joy and holy lays,
  Thy Guide and Shepherd True;

2 Dare all thou canst, yea, take thy fill
Of praise and adoration, still
  Thou fail'st to reach His due.

3 A special theme for thankful hearts,
The Bread that lives, and life imparts,
  To-day is duly set;

4 Which at the solemn festal board,
Was dealt around, when, with their Lord,
  His chosen Twelve were met.

5 Full be the praise and sweetly sounding,
With joy and reverence meet abounding,
  The soul's glad festival;

6 Dies enim solémnis ágitur,
  In quæ mensæ prima recólitur
  Hujus institútio.

7 In hac mensa novi Regis,
  Novum pascha novæ legis
  Phase vetus términat.

8 Vetustátem nóvitas,
  Umbram fugat véritas,
  Noctem lux elíminat.

9 Quod in cœna Christus gessit,
  Faciéndum hoc expréssit
  In Sui memóriam.

10 Docti sacris institútis
   Panem, vinum in salútis
   Consecrámus hóstiam.

11 Dogma datur Christiánis,
   Quod in carnem transit panis,
   Et vinem in sánguinem.

12 Quod non capis, quod non vides,
   Animósa firmat fides
   Præter rerum órdinem.

13 Sub divérsis speciébus,
   Signis tantum et non rebus,
   Latent res exímiæ.

6 This is the day of glorious state,
When of that Feast we celebrate
   The high original.

7 'Tis here our King makes all things new,
And living rules and offerings true
   Absorb each legal right;

8 Before the new retreats the old,
And life succeeds to shadows cold,
   And day displaces night.

9 His faithful followers Christ hath bid
To do what at the Feast He did,
   For sweet remembrance' sake;

10 And, gifted through His high commands,
Of bread and wine their priestly hands
   A saving Victim make.

11 O Truth to Christian love display'd,
The bread His Very Body made,
   His Very Blood the wine;

12 Nor eye beholds, nor thought conceives,
But dauntless Faith the change believes
   Wrought by a pow'r Divine.

13 Beneath two diff'ring species
(Signs only, not their substances,)
   Lie mysteries deep and rare;

14 Caro cibus, sanguis potus :
  Manet tamen Christus totus
    Sub utráque spécie.

15 A suménte non concísus
  Non confráctus non divísus,
    Integer accípitur.

16 Sumit unus, sumunt mille
  Quantum isti, tantum ille
    Nec sumptus consúmitur.

17 Sumunt boni, sumunt mali :
  Sorte tamen inæquáli,
    Vitæ vel intéritus.

18 Mors est malis, vita bonis,
  Vide paris sumptiónis,
    Quam sit dispar éxitus.

19 Fracto demum Sacraménto,
  Ne vacilles, sed meménto,
    Tantum esse sub fragménto
      Quantum toto tégitur.

20 Nulla rei fit scissúra :
  Signi tantum fit fractúra :
    Qua, nec status nec statúra
      Signáti minúitur.

14 His Flesh the meat, the drink His Blood,
   Yet Christ entire, our heav'nly Food,
     Beneath each kind is there.

15 And they who of the Lord partake,
   Nor sever Him, nor rend, nor break,
     All gain, and nought is lost;

16 The boon now one, now thousands claim,
   Yet one and all receive the Same,
     Receive, but ne'er exhaust.

17 The Gift is shar'd by all, yet tends,
   In bad and good, to diff'ring ends
     Of blessing, or of woe;

18 What death to some, salvation brings
   To others; lo! from common springs
     What various issues flow!

19 Nor be thy faith confounded, though
   The Sacrament be broke; for know,
   The life which in the whole doth glow
     In ev'ry part remains;

20 No force the Substance can divide,
   Which those meek forms terrestrial hide,
   The Sign is broke; the signified
     Nor change nor loss sustains.

21 Ecce panis Angelórum,
    Factus cibus viatórum :
    Vere panis filiórum :
        Non mitténdus cánibus.

22 In figúris præsignátur
    Cum Isaac inmolátur ;
    Agnus Paschæ deputátur
        Datur Manna pátribus.

23 Bone Pastor, panis vere,
    Jesu nostri miserére :
    Tu nos pasce, nos tuére,
    Tu nos bona fac vidére
        In terra vivéntium,

24 Tu qui cuncta scis et vales,
    Qui nos pascis hic mortáles :
    Tuos ibi commensáles,
    Cohærédes et sodáles
    Fac sanctórum cívium.
                Amen—Allcluia.

---

119. *O Salutaris Hostia,*

1 O salutáris Hóstia,
    Quæ cœli pándis óstium
    Bella premunt hostília,
    Da róbur, fer auxílium.

21 The Bread of Angels, lo ! is sent
 For weary pilgrims' nourishment ;
 The children's Bread, not to be spent
  On worthless dogs profane ;

22 In types significant portray'd,
 Young Isaac on the altar laid,
 And paschal offerings duly made,
  And manna's fruitful rain.

23 O Thou Good Shepherd, Very Bread,
 Jesu, on us Thy mercy shed ;
  Sweetly feed us,
  Gently·lead us,
 Till of Thy Fulness us Thou give
 Safe in the land of them that live.

24 Thou who canst all, and all dost know,
 Thou who dost feed us here below,
  Grant us to share
  Thy banquet there,
 Co-heirs and partners of Thy love
 With the blest citizens above.
  Amen, Alleluia.

———

120. *O Saving Victim !*

O saving Victim ! opening wide
The gate of Heaven to man below !
Our foes press on from every side ;
Thine aid supply, Thy strength bestow.

2 Uni Trinoque Domino
Sit sempiterna glória,
Qui vitam sine término
Nobis donet in pátria.
Amen.

----

121. *Pange Lingua.*

Pange lingua gloriósi
Corporis mystérium,
Sanguinisque pretiósi,
Quem in mundi pretium
Fructus ventris generósi
Rex effudit gentium.

Nobis datus, nobis nátus
Ex intacta Vírgine
Et in mundo conversátus
Sparso verbi sémine
Sui moras incolátus
Miro clausit ordine.

In suprémæ noctæ cœnæ
Recumbens cum frátribus
Observata lege plene
Cibis in legálibus
Cibum turbæ duodénæ
Se dat suis manibus.

Verbum cáro pánem vérum
Verbo carnem efficit
Fitque sanguis Christe merum

2 To Thy great Name, be endless praise,
 Immortal Godhead, One in Three!
Oh grant us endless length of days,
 In our true native land, with Thee!

---

122.   *Sing, my tongue, the Saviour's glory.*

Sing, my tongue, the Saviour's glory,
 Of His Flesh the mystery sing;
Of the Blood, all price exceeding,
 Shed by our Immortal King,
Destin'd for the world's Redemption,
 From a noble womb to spring.

Of a pure and spotless Virgin
 Born for us on earth below,
He, as Man with man conversing,
 Stay'd, the seeds of truth to sow;
Then He clos'd in solemn order
 Wondrously His life of woe.

On the night of that Last Supper,
 Seated with His chosen band,
He the paschal victim eating,
 First fulfils the Law's command;
Then, as Food to all His brethren,
 Gives Himself with His own hand.

Word made Flesh, the bread of nature
 By His word to Flesh He turns;
Wine into His Blood He changes:—
11

Et si sensus déficit
Ad firmadum cor sincérum
Sola fides sufficit.

Tantum ergo Sácramentum
Venerémur cernui :
Et antíquum documentum
Novo cedat ritui :
Præstet fides supplementum
Sensuum defectui.

Genitóri Genitóque
Laus et Jubilátio
Salus honor virtus quoque
Sit et benedictio :
Procedenti ab utróque
Compar sit laudátio.

---

123. *Litaniæ B. Mariæ Virginis.*

Kyrie eléison.
Kyrie eléison.
Christe eléison.
Christe eléison.
Kyrie eléison.
Kyrie eléison.
Christe audi nos.
Christe exaúdi nos.
Pater de cœlis Deus,

Miserére nobis.

Fili Redémptor mundi Deus,

Spíritus Sancte Deus,

Sancta Trínitas, unus Deus,

Miserére nobis.

Sancta María,
Ora pro nobis.
Sancta Dei Génitrix,
Ora pro nobis.

What though sense no change discerns!
Only be the heart in earnest,
 Faith her lesson quickly learns.

Down in adoration falling,
 Lo! the Sacred Host we hail:
Lo! o'er ancient forms departing,
 Newer rites of grace prevail:
Faith for all defects supplying,
 Where the feeble senses fail.

To the Everlasting Father,
 And the Son who reigns on high,
With the Holy Ghost proceeding
 Forth from Each eternally,
Be Salvation, Honour, Blessing;
 Might and endless Majesty.

---

124 *Litany of the Blessed Virgin.*

Lord have mercy.
Lord have mercy.
Christ have mercy.
Christ have mercy.
Lord have mercy.
Lord have mercy.
Christ hear us.
Christ graciously hear us.
God, the Father of heaven,
Have mercy on us.

God the Son, Redeemer of the world,
God, the Holy Ghost,
Holy Trinity, one God,
 Have mercy on us.

Holy Mary,
Pray for us.
Holy Mother of God,
Pray for us.

Sancta Virgo Vírginum,
Mater Christi,
Mater divínæ gratiæ,
Mater puríssima,
Mater castíssima,
Mater inviláta,
Mater intemeráta,
Mater amábilis,

Mater admirábilis,

Mater Creatóris,

Mater Salvatóris,

Virgo prudentíssima,
Virgo veneránda,

Virgo prædicánda,

Virgo pótens,

Vírgo clémens,

Virgo fidélis,

Spéculum justítiæ,
Sedes sapientiæ,

Ora pro nobis.

Causa nostræ lætítiæ,
Vas spirituále,
Vas honorábile,
Vas insigne devotiónis,
Rosa mystica,
Turris Davídica,
Turris ebúrnea,
Domus aúrea,
Fœderis arca,

Janua cœli,
Stella matutína,
Salus infirmórum,
Refugium peccatórum,
Consolatrix afflictórum,
Auxilium Christianórum,
Regína Angelórum,
Regína Patriarchárum,
Regína Prophetárum,
Regína Apostórum,
Regína Mártyrum,
Regína Confessórum,
Regína Vírginum,

Ora pro nobis.

Holy Virgin of vir-
gins,
Mother of Christ,
Mother of divine
grace,
Mother most pure,
Mother most chaste,
Mother inviolate,
Mother undefiled,
Mother most ami-
able,
Mother most ad-
mirable,
Mother of our Cre-
ator,
Mother of our Sa-
viour,
Virgin most pru-
dent,
Virgin most vene-
rable,
Virgin most re-
nowned,
Virgin most power-
ful,
Virgin most merci-
ful,
Virgin most faith-
ful,
Mirror of justice,
Seat of Wisdom,

Pray for us.

Cause of our joy,

Spiritual vessel,
Vessel of honour,
Vessel of singular
devotion,
Mystical Rose,
Tower of David,
Tower of Ivory,
House of Gold,
Ark of the Cove-
nant,
Gate of Heaven,
Morning Star,
Health of the sick,
Refuge of sinners,

Comforter of the
afflicted,
Help of Christians,

Queen of Angels,
Queen of Patri-
archs,
Queen of Prophets,

Queen of Apostles,
Queen of Martyrs,
Queen of Confess-
ors,
Queen of Virgins,

Pray for us.

Regína Sanctórum om-   Agnus Dei, qui tollis
nium,   peccáta mundi,
Ora pro nobis.
Regína sine labe origi-   *Exaúdi nos, Dómine.*
náli concepta,
Ora pro nobis.   Agnus Dei, qui tollis
Agnus Dei, qui tollis   peccáta mundi,
peccáta mundi,
                             Miserére nobis.
Parce nobis, Dómine.

---

125. *Alma Redemptoris Mater.*

Alma Redemptória Mater, quæ pervia cœli
Porta mánes, et Stella máris, succúrre cadénti,
Surgere qui cúrat, populo : tu quæ genuísti,
Natura mirante, tuum sanctum Genitórem ;
Virgo prius ac posterius, Gabrielis ab ore,
Sumens illud Ave, peccatorum miserere.

---

127 *Ave Regina.*

Ave, Regína cœlorum !
Ave, dómina angelórum !
Salve, rádix, salve, porta,
Ex quâ mundo Lúx est orta.

Queen of all Saints,

Pray for us.

Queen, conceived with-
out original sin,

Pray for us.

Lamb of God, who
takest away the sins
of the world :

Spare us, O Lord !

Lamb of God, who
takest away the sins
of the world,

*Graciously hear us, O
Lord !*

Lamb of God who
takest away the sins
of the world :

Have mercy on us.

Christ hear us.

Christ graciously hear us.

---

126. *Mother of Christ.*

Mother of Christ! hear thou thy people's cry,
Star of the deep, and Portal of the sky !
Mother of Him who thee from nothing made,
Sinking we strive, and call to thee for aid:
Oh, by that joy which Gabriel brought to thee,
Thou Virgin first and last, let us thy mercy see.

---

128. *Hail, O Queen of Heaven.*

Hail, O Queen of Heav'n enthron'd !
Hail, by angels mistress own'd,
Root of Jesse, gate of morn,
Whence the world's true light was born.

Gaude, Vírgo gloriósa,
Super omnes speciósa.
Vale, O valde decóra!
Et pro nóbis Christum exora.

---

129. *Regina cœli.*

Regína cœli, lætáre! allelúia.
Quia quem meruísti portare; allelúia.
Resurrexit sicut dixit; allelúia.
Ora pro nobis Deum; allelúia.

---

131. *Salve Regina.*

Salve, Regína, mater misericórdiæ;
Vita, dulcédo, et spes nostra, salve.
Ad te clamamus, exules, filii Hevæ.
Ad te suspirámus gementes et flentes in hac
lacrymarum valle.
Eia ergo, Advocáta nostra,
Illos tuos misericórdes óculos ad nos convérte;
Et Jesum benedíctum fructum ventris tui,
Nobis post hoc exilium osténde,
O clemens, O pia, O dulcis Virgo Maria.

Glorious Virgin, joy to thee,
Joy and endless Jubilee;
Fairest thou where all are fair!
Plead with Christ our sins to spare.

---

130. *Joy to thee.*

Joy to thee, O Queen of Heaven! alleluia.
He whom thou wast meet to bear; alleluia.
As He promised, hath arisen; alleluia.
Pour for us to Him thy prayer: alleluia.

---

132. *Salve Regina.*

Mother of Mercy, hail, O gentle Queen!
Our life, our sweetness, and our hope, all hail!
Children of Eve,
To thee we cry from our sad banishment;
To thee we send our sighs,
Weeping and mourning in this tearful vale.
Come then, our Advocate;
Oh, turn on us those pitying eyes of thine:
And our long exile past,
Shew us at last
Jesus, of thy pure womb the fruit divine.
O Virgin Mary, mother blest!
O sweetest, gentlest, holiest!

133. *Ave Maris Stella.*

1 Ave maris stella,
  Dei Mater alma,
  Atque semper virgo,
  Felix cœli porta.

2 Sumens illud Ave
  Gabriélis ore,
  Funda nos in pace,
  Mutans Hevæ nomen.

3 Solve vincla reis,
  Profer lumen cæcis,
  Mala nostra pelle,
  Bona cuncta posce.

4 Monstra te esse matrem,
  Sumat per te preces,
  Qui pro nobis natus,
  Tulit esse tuus.

5 Virgo singuláris,
  Inter omnes mitis,
  Nos culpis solútos,
  Mites fac et castos.

6 Vitam præsta puram,
  Iter para tutum,
  Ut vidéntes Jesum,
  Semper collætémur

134. *Hail! thou Star of Ocean.*

1 Hail, thou Star of Ocean!
 Portal of the sky!
Ever Virgin Mother
 Of the Lord most High!

2 Oh! by Gabriel's Ave,
 Uttered long ago,
Eva's name reversing,
 'Stablish peace below.

3 Break the captive's fetters,
 Light on blindness pour;
All our ills expelling,
 Every bliss implore.

4 Show thyself a mother;
 Offer Him our sighs,
Who for us Incarnate
 Did not thee despise.

5 Virgin of all virgins!
 To thy shelter take us:
Gentlest of the gentle!
 Chaste and gentle make us.

6 Still as on we journey
 Help our weak endeavour;
Till with thee and Jesus
 We rejoice for ever.

7 Sit laus Deo Patri
  Summo Christo decus,
    Spirítui Sancto,
    Tribus honor unus.   Amen.

---

135. *Stabat Mater.*

1 Stabat Mater dolorósa
  Juxta crucem lacrymósa,
    Dum pendébat Fílius.
  Cujus ánimam geméntem,
  Contristátam, et doléntem,
    Pertransívit gládius.

2 O quam tristis et afflícta
  Fuit illa benedícta
    Mater Unigéniti!
  Quæ mœrébat, et dolébat,
  Pia Mater, dum vidébat
    Nati pœnas ínclyti.

3 Quis est homo qui non fleret,
  Matrem Christi si vidéret
    In tanto supplício?
  Quis non posset contristári,
  Christi Matrem contemplári
    Doléntem cum Fílio?

4 Pro peccátis suæ gentis
  Vidit Jesum in torméntis,
    Et flagéllis súbditum.

7 Through the highest heaven,
   To the Almighty Three,
Father, Son and Spirit,
   One same glory be.

———

136. *Stabat Mater.*

1 The pious Mother mourned her loss ;
  She stood and wept beneath the cross,
    Which bore her much-loved Son :
  And through her deeply wounded breast,
  With sorrow's heaviest weight oppressed
    The sword of grief was run.

2 Then how full of deep-felt anguish,
  Did that blessed Mother languish,
    For Him her only love !
  With trembling and with sadness worn,
  How deeply did that Mother mourn
    His pangs, Who bled above.

3 Where is the man, who all unmoved,
  Could see her, who so truly loved,
    Thus sunk in bitter grief?
  The painful scene who could have borne,
  So pure a soul with anguish torn,
    And none to yield relief?

4 She saw His blood profusely shed,
  For His own people's crimes He bled,
    From stripes and cruel blows:

Vidit suum dulcem Natum
Moriéndo desolátum,
  Dum emísit spíritum.

5 Eia Mater, fons amóris,
Me sentíre vim dolóris
  Fac, ut tecum lúgeam.
Fac ut árdeat cor meum
In amándo Christum Deum,
  Ut sibi compláceam.

6 Sancta Mater, istud agas,
Crucifíxi fige plagas
  Cordi meo válide.
Tui Nati vulneráti,
Tam dignáti pro me pati,
  Pœnas mecum dívide.

7 Fac me tecum pie flere,
Crucifíxo condolére,
  Donec ego víxero
Juxta crucem tecum stare,
Et me tibi sociáre
  In planctu desídero.

8 Virgo vírginum præclára,
Mihi jam non sis amára;
  Fac me tecum plángere.
Fac ut portem Christi mortem
Passiónis fac consórtem,
  Et plagas recólere.

She saw her sweet and only child,
In desolation calm and mild,
   In life's expiring throes.

5 Hear then, O mother! source of love,
Let me thy bitter sorrows prove,
   And let me weep with thee.
May my poor heart be all on fire,
With Christ's bright love, let my desire
   To please Him ever be.

6 Let His wounds make deep impression
Let them hold a sweet possession
   Firm in my faithful heart;
Let no joys my fond love sever;
In His pains O let me ever
   Suffer with thee a part,

7 O make me truly weep with thee;
Mourning with Him who died for me,
   Let me in grief expire:
By His loved cross, with thee to stay,
With thee to tread thy painful way,
   Such is my fond desire.

8 Virgin, above all virgins blest!
All my poor longing heart's request
   Is with thy grief to mourn:
O may I bear my Saviour's death,
Treasuring until my latest breath,
   All that His love has borne.

9 Fac me plagis vulnerári
    Fac me Cruce inebriári,
      Et crúore Fílii.
    Flammis ne urar succénsus,
    Per te, Virgo, sim defénsus
      In die judícii.

10 Christe, cum sit hinc exíre,
    Da per Matrem me veníre
      Ad palmam victóriæ.
    Quando corpus moriétur,
    Fac ut únimæ donétur
      Paradísi gloria.   Amen.

———

137. *Magnificat.*

Magníficat ánima mea Dóminum.
Et exultavit spíritus meus : in Deo salutári **meo.**

Quia respexit humilitátem ancillæ suæ : **ecce**
enim ex hoc beátam me dicent omnes generá-
tiones.

Quia fecit mihi magna qui potens est : **et**
sanctum nómen ejus.

Et misericórdia ejus a progenie in progenies :
timentibus eum.

Fecit potentiam in brachio suo : dispersit supér-
bos mente cordis sui.

Depósuit poténtes de séde : et exaltávit húmiles.

9 Let me my Saviour's sufferings share,
And His sweet cross devoutly bear,
For thy own Son's pure love :
And burning with love's holy fire,
O screen me from the vengeful ire
Of my great Judge above.

10 May the bright cross my guardian be,
My Saviour's death, defence for me,
And source of every grace.
And when my body meets decay,
Obtain my soul in that dread day,
In paradise a place.   Amen.

---

138. *The Magnificat, or Canticle of the Blessed Virgin.*

My soul doth magnify : the Lord.

And my spirit hath rejoiced : in God my Saviour.

For He hath regarded the humility of His handmaid : for behold from henceforth all generations shall call me blessed.

For He that is mighty hath done great things unto me : and Holy is His Name.

And His mercy is from generation to generation : unto them that fear Him.

He hath shewed strength with His arm : He hath scattered the proud in the imagination of their hearts.

He hath put down the mighty from their seat: and hath exalted the humble.

12

Esuriéntes implévit bonis : et divites dimísit inánes.

Suscépit Israel púerum suum : recordátus misericórdiæ suæ.

Sicut locútus est ad pátres nostros : Abraham, et sémini ejus in sæcula.

Gloria Patri, &c.

---

139. *Te Deum laudamus.*

Te Deum laudámus : Te Dóminum confitémur.

Te ætérnum Patrem : omnis terra veneratur.

Tibi omnes Angeli : Tibi cœli, et univérsæ potestátes.

Tibi Chérubim et Séraphim : incessábili voce proclámant :

Sanctus, Sanctus, Sanctus : Dóminus Deus Sábaoth :

Pleni sunt cœli et terra : majestátis glóriæ tuæ.

Te gloriósus : Apostolórum chorus.

Te Prophetárum : laudábilis númerus.

Te Mártyrum candidátus : laudat exércitus.

Te per orbem terrárum : sancta confitétur Ecclésia.

Patrem : imménsæ majestátis.

Venerándum tuum verum : et únicum Filium.

Sanctum quoque : Paráclitum Spíritum.

He hath filled the hungry with good things :
but the rich He hath sent empty away.

He hath upholden His servant Israel : being
mindful of His mercy.

As He spake unto our fathers : to Abraham
and his seed for ever.

Glory be to the Father, &c.

---

140. *We praise Thee, O God.*

We praise Thee, O God: we acknowledge
Thee to be the Lord.

All the earth doth worship Thee: the Father
everlasting.

To Thee all angels cry aloud, the heavens and
all the powers therein :

To Thee cherubim and seraphim : continually
do cry:

Holy, Holy, Holy : Lord God of Sabaoth.

Heaven and earth are full: of the majesty of
Thy glory.

The glorious choir of the Apostles : praise Thee.

The admirable company of the Prophets:
praise Thee.

The white-robed army of Martyrs : praise Thee.

The Holy Church throughout all the world:
doth acknowledge Thee.

The Father : of an infinite majesty.

Thy adorable, true: and only Son.

Also the Holy Ghost: the Comforter.

Tu Rex glóriæ : Christe.
Tu Patris: sempitérnus es Fílius.
Tu ad liberándum susceptúrus hóminem : non
horruisti Vírginis úterum.
Tu· devícto mortis acúleo : aperuísti credéntibus
regna cœlórum.

Tu ad déxteram Dei sedes : in glória Patris.

Judex créderis : esse ventúrus.

* Te ergo quæsumus, tuis fámulis súbveni :
quos pretióso sánguine redemísti.

Ætérna fac cum Sanctis Tuis: in glória numerári.

Salvum fac pópulum tuum, Dómine · et béne-
dic hæreditáti tuæ.
Et rege eos : et extólle illos, usque in ætérnum.
Per singulos dies : benedícimus te
Et laudámus nomen tuum in sæculum : et in
sæculum sæculi.
Dignáre Dómine, die isto : sine peccáto nos
custodíre.
Miserére nostri, Dómine : miserére nostri.

Fiat misericórdia tua, Dómine, super nos :
quemádmodum sperávimus in te.
  In te, Dómine, sperávi : non confúndar in
ætérnum.

* Here all kneel.

Thou art the King of Glory : O Christ.

Thou art the everlasting Son : of the Father.

When Thou tookest upon Thee to deliver man : Thou didst not abhor the Virgin's womb.

When Thou hadst overcome the sting of death : Thou didst open the kingdom of heaven to all believers.

Thou sittest at the right hand of God : in the glory of the Father.

We believe that Thou shalt come : to be our Judge.

* We pray Thee, therefore, help Thy servants : whom Thou hast redeemed with Thy precious blood.

Make them to be numbered with Thy Saints : in glory everlasting.

O Lord, save Thy people : and bless Thine inheritance.

Govern them : and lift them up for ever.

Day by day : we magnify Thee.

And we praise Thy name for ever : yea, for ever and ever.

Vouchsafe, O Lord, this day : to keep us without sin.

O Lord, have mercy upon us : have mercy upon us.

O Lord, let Thy mercy be shewed upon us : as we have hoped in Thee.

O Lord, in Thee have I hoped : let me not be confounded for ever.

* Here all kneel.

141. *Miserere.*

Miserere mei, Deus: secúndum magnam miseric'rdiam tuam.

Et secúndum multitúdinem miseratiónum tuárum: dele iniquitátem meam.

Amplius lava me ab iniquitáte mea: et a peccáto meo munda me.

Quoniam iniquitátem meam ego cognósco: et peccátum meum contra me est semper.

Tibi soli peccávi, et malum coram te feci: ut justificéris in sermónibus tuis, et vincas cum judic'ris.

Ecce enim in iniquitátibus concéptus sum: et in peccátis concèpit me mater mea.

Ecce enim veritátem dilexísti: incérta et occúlta sapiéntiæ tuæ, manifestásti mihi.

Aspérges me hyssópo, et mundábor; lavábis me, et super nivem dealbábor.

Audítui meo dabis gaudium et lætítiam: et exultábunt ossa humiliáta.

Avérte fáciem tuam a peccátis meis; et omnes iniquitátes meas dele.

Cor mundum crea in me, Deus: et spíritum rectum ínnova in viscéribus meis.

Ne projícias me a fácie tua: et Spíritum sanctum tuum ne aúferas a me.

Redde mihi lætítiam salutáris tui: et spíritu principáli confirma me.

142. *Miserere.*

Have mercy upon me, O God : according to Thy great mercy.

And according to the multitude of Thy tender mercies : blot out my iniquity.

Wash me yet more from my iniquity : and cleanse me from my sin.

For I acknowledge my iniquity : and my sin is always before me.

Against Thee only have I sinned, and done evil in Thy sight : that Thou mayest be justified in Thy words, and mayest overcome when Thou art judged.

For behold, I was conceived in iniquities, and in sins did my mother conceive me.

For behold, Thou hast loved truth : the uncertain and hidden things of Thy wisdom Thou hast made manifest unto me.

Thou shalt sprinkle me with hyssop, and I shall be cleansed : Thou shalt wash me, and I shall be made whiter than snow.

Thou shalt make me hear of joy and gladness: and the bones that were humbled shall rejoice.

Turn away Thy face from my sins : and blot out all my iniquities.

Create in me a clean heart, O God : and renew a right spirit within my bowels.

Cast me not away from Thy presence : and take not thy holy Spirit from me.

Restore unto me the joy of Thy salvation : and strengthen me with a perfect spirit.

Docébo iníquos vias tuas: et ímpii ad te converténtur. ·

Líbera me de sanguínibus, Deus Deus salútis meæ: et exultábit lingua mea justitiam tuam.

Dómine, lábia mea apéries: et os meum annuntiábit laudem tuam.

Quoniam si voluísses sacrifícium, dedíssem útique: holocaústis non delectáberis.

Sacrifícium Deo spíritus contribulátus: cor contrítum et humiliátum, Deus, non despícies.

Benígne fac, Dómine, in bona voluntáte tua Sion: ut ædificéntur muri Jerúsalem.

Tunc acceptábis sacrifícium justítiæ, oblatiónes, et holocaústa: tunc impónent super altáre tuum vítulos.

Gloria, &c.

___

143. *De Profundis.*

De profúndis clamávi ad te, Dómine: Dómine, exaúdi vocem meam.

Fiant aures tuæ intendéntes: in vocem deprecatiónis meæ.

Si iniquitátes observáveris, Dómine: Dómine, quis sustinébit?

Quia apud te propitiátio est: et propter legem tuam sustínui te, Dómine.

I will teach the unjust Thy ways : and the wicked shall be converted unto Thee.

Deliver me from bloodguiltiness, O God, Thou God of my salvation : and my tongue shall extol Thy justice.

Thou shalt open my lips, O Lord : and my mouth shall declare Thy praise.

For if Thou hadst desired sacrifice, I would surely have given it : with burnt offerings Thou wilt not be delighted.

The sacrifice of God is an afflicted spirit : a contrite and humble heart, O God, Thou wilt not despise.

Deal favourably, O Lord, in Thy good will with Sion : that the walls of Jerusalem may be built up.

Then shalt Thou accept the sacrifice of justice, oblations, and whole burnt-offerings : then shall they lay calves upon Thine altars.

Glory be to the Father, &c.

---

144. *De Profundis.*

Out of the depths have I cried unto Thee, O Lord : Lord, hear my voice.

Oh, let Thine ears consider well : the voice of my supplication.

If Thou, O Lord, shalt mark iniquities : Lord, who shall abide it?

For with Thee there is propitiation : and because of Thy law I have waited for Thee, O Lord.

Sustínuit ánima mea in verbo ejus :   sperávit ánima·mea in Dómino.

A custódia matutína usque ad noctem : speret Israel in Dómino.

Quia apud Dóminum misericórdia : et copiósa apud eum redémptio.

Et ipse rèdimet Israel, ex ómnibus iniquitátibus ejus.

Réquiem ætérnam dona eis Dómine.
Et lux perpétua lúceat eis.

My soul hath waited on His word: my soul hath hoped in the Lord.

From the morning watch even until night: let Israel hope in the Lord.

For with the Lord there is mercy: and with Him is plenteous Redemption.

And He shall redeem Israel from all his iniquities.

Eternal rest give to them, O Lord.
And let perpetual light shine on them.

PRINTED BY RICHARDSON AND SON, DERBY.

𝔍. 𝔐. 𝔍.

—

MUSIC

FOR THE

HOLY FAMILY
HYMNS.

WITH THE APPROBATION OF
HIS EMINENCE CARDINAL WISEMAN.

LONDON:
RICHARDSON AND SON,
26, PATERNOSTER ROW; 9, CAPEL STREET, DUBLIN;
AND DERBY.
1860.

INDEX FOR THE TUNES.*

* The hymns marked thus † are sung to the melodies of
other hymns.

LATIN HYMNS.

NOTICE,

I. The *time* and *expression* marked on the tunes, should be observed, and special care taken *not to sing them too fast.*

II. To reduce the number of tunes, in some cases several Hymns are set to the same.

III. All the tunes for the Latin pieces, of this collection have not been printed here, but may be found in " Gregorian Hymns for Vespers " by the Rev. W. I. Dolan—Messrs. Burns and Lambert, and in Webbe's Music—Mr. Novello, &c.

IV. The Harmonies of these tunes will be printed if found necessary.

V. Any observation concerning the improvement of these Hymns will be received thankfully.

HOLY FAMILY HYMNS.

I. ALMIGHTY GOD.

1. *The Most Holy Trinity.*

Adagio.

Have mer - cy on us, God Most High! Who
lift our hearts to Thee; Have mercy on us
worms of earth, Most Ho - ly Tri - ni - ty!

2. *The Earth is the Lord's.*

Tune No. 1,

3. *Thanksgiving.*

CHORUS. *Moderato.*

Be - ne - dic - tion and praise, From our

hearts let us   raise   To this   Lord of   grace and

FINE.

love,   To this   Lord of   grace and   love.

SOLO.

Praise   we   our   God   with   joy   And

glad-ness   ne - ver   end - ing;   An - gels and

D. C.

Saints with   us   Their grateful voices   blend - ing.

---

4. Thanksgiving.

(Choral Symphony of Beethoven.)

Cantabile.

Praise we our   God with joy And   glad - ness ne - ver

end - ing: An - gels and   Saints with us Their

FINE.

grate ful voices blend - ing. Thanks and bless - ing,

D. C.

Past ex - press-ing, To this ten - der Lord are due.

———————

HOLY GHOST.

5.   *Holy Ghost come down.*

Moderato.   CHORUS.

Ho - ly   Ghost, come down up - on Thy

children, Give us   grace, and make us   Thine; Thy ten - der

fires with - in us   kin - dle, Blessed   Spi - rit! Dove Di-

vine! Thy ten - der   fires within us   kin - dle, Blessed

FINE.   SOLO.

Spi - rit Dove Di - vine!   For all with-

In us good and ho - ly Is from

Thee, Thy pre - cious gift, In all our joys in all our

D. C.

sor - rows, Wist - ful hearts to Thee we lift.

6. *Holy Spirit, grant our prayer,*

Moderato. CHORUS.

Ho - ly Spi - rit, grant our pray'r, In -

flame our te - pid hearts, With Thy in - spir - ing darts;

Ho - ly Spirit grant our pray'r, In - flame our tepid hearts, Make Thy

FINE. SOLO 1st, for Stanza 1 and 3.

dwell-ing there. Of all gifts, Thou Giv - er art,

In Thy trea-sures give us part; Grant the prayer we pray, To

D. C. *Chorus.* SOLO 2nd, for Stanza 2 and 4.

Thee this day. In Thy ab - sence vain - ly shine The

stores of gifts di - vine, Like a dia mond mine;
D. C.

Kept from Thee our heart is sure to smart.

7. *Send forth Thy Light, O Lord.*

SOLO. *With Spirit.*

What fire is this with-in my breast? What God, in-

ha - bi - ting my soul? Thou Giv - er

of the end - less rest In a - do - ra-tion low I

CHORUS. F

kneel, E - ter - nal Glad - ness un - ex-pressed! Send

forth Thy light, O   Lord,   And keep us in Thy   grace; Un-

til in Heav'n we   see The bright-ness of Thy   face.

8. *O Holy Ghost, on us descend.*

CHORUS. *Moderato.*

Oh! Ho - ly Ghost on us de - scend, Thy Spi - rit

with our souls to blend. Inspire our hearts with burning love, And to

us all Thy good - ness prove, In-spire our hearts with burn-ing

FINE.

love; And to   us all Thy good - ness   prove.

FIRST SOLO.

With - out Thee   all is   va - ni - ty, Where Thou art

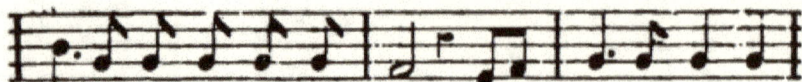

not we wan-der all a - stray; Oh! dis-si-pate our

ig - no - rance, we pray, Oh dis - si - pate our

ig-no-rance we pray, Pro -tect us with Thy e - ver watch - ful

D. C. SECOND SOLO.

eye. (*Chorus.*) Hell's de - mons all en - dea - vour to de -

stroy The faith - ful by this world's se - duc - tive

snare, To un - der - mine our heart's ce - les - tial

joy. Be Thou our heav'n-ly Sov - er - eign and

D. C.

Guide, All sin to cure, all sor-row to re-pair. (*Chorus.*)

THIRD SOLO.

Teach us Thy hea-venly wis-dom, Lord, we pray, For that a-

lone our mor-tal life can bless; 'Tis in that

path the young their mirth dis - play, And old age

D. C.

dwells in peace-ful hap-pi - ness. (Chorus.)

II. OUR BLESSED LORD.

THE SACRED INFANCY.

9. Christmas Hymn.

SOLO. Moderately.

The An-gels we have heard on high, Most

sweet-ly sing-ing o'er our plains, And still the moun-tains

in re-ply Are e-cho-ing their joy-ous strains:

CHORUS F.

Glo - - - - - - - - - ri - a

in ex - cel - sis De - o.　Glo - - - - - -

a - - ri - a　in ex-cel-sis　De - o.

10. *The Infant Saviour.*

SOLO. *Cheerfully.*

See a - mid the win-ter's snow, Born for us on

earth be - low, See, the ten - der Lamb ap-pears, Pro-mis'd

CHORUS.

from e - ter-nal years! Hail, thou e - ver bless-ed morn!

Hail Re - demp-tion's hap-py dawn! Sing thro' all Je -

ru-sa - lem,   Christ is   born in   Beth-le - hem.

11. *Jesus and Mary.*

Cantabile. SOLO. P.

Oft as   Thee, my   in - fant   Saviour,

In Thy mo-ther's arms I   view, Straight a   thou - sand

thrill-ing rap-tures O - ver - flow my   heart   a - new.

CHORUS F.

Hap-py Babe! and   hap - py   mo-ther!   O how great your

bliss   must be!   Each en - fold-ed   in   the o - ther,

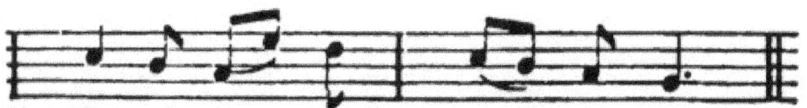

Sip - ping pure   fe - li - ci - ty!

12. *Dear Little One.*

Moderato.

Dear - Lit - tle One! how sweet Thou art, Thine

eyes how bright they shine, So bright they al - most

seem to speak When Ma - ry's look meets Thine. How

faint and fee - ble is Thy cry, Like plaint of harm-less

dove, When Thou dost mur - mur * in Thy sleep Of

sor - row and of love, Of sor - row and of love.

---

13. *The Infant Jesus asleep.*

P. Soft and Slow.

Sleep, Ho - ly Babe, Up - on Thy mo - ther's

breast! Great Lord of earth and sea and sky,

How sweet it is to see Thee lie

In such a place of rest!

Rallentando.

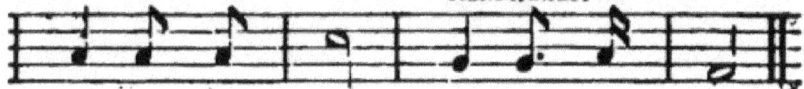

Sleep, Ho - ly Babe! Sleep, Ho - ly Babe!

---

14. *The Infant Jesus in the crib,*

Tune No. 90,

---

15. *The Epiphany.*

Tune No. 20.

THE PASSION,

16. *Hail Wounds!*

Tune No. 18.

17. *' O'erwhelm'd in depths of woe.'*

Andante.

O'er - whelm'd in depths of woe,

Up - on the tree of scorn,

Hangs the Re - deem - er of man-

kind With rack - ing an - guish torn.

18. *The Passion of Jesus.*

SOLO.

My Je - sus! say, what wretch has dared, Thy

sa - cred hands to bind? And who has dared to

CHORUS.

buf fet so, Thy face so meek and kind? 'Tis

I have thus un-grate-ful been, Yet Je-sus pi-ty take! Oh!

spare and par-don me, my Lord, For Thy sweet mer-cy's sake.

19. *Jesus Crucified.*

Oh! come and mourn with me   a while; See,

Ma-ry calls us   to her side; Oh!   come and   let us

mourn with her; Je-sus, our Love,   is   cru-ci-fied!

THE RESURRECTION.

20. *Jesus Risen.*

With Spirit.

All hail! dear Con-que-ror!   All   Hail!

O what a vic-to-ry is Thine! How beau-ti-

ful Thy strength ap - pears, Thy crim-son wounds how

bright they shine! How beau-ti-ful Thy strength ap-

pears, Thy crim-son wounds how bright they shine.

THE BLESSED SACRAMENT.

21. Sweet Sacrament.

SOLO.

Je-sus! my Lord, my God, my all!

How can I love Thee as I ought? And how re-

vere this won-drous gift, So far sur-pass-ing

hope or thought? Sweet Sa-cra - ment ! we   Thee a-

dore! Oh! make us   love thee   more   and   more!

22. *The Elevation of the Host:*

SOLO. *Solema,*

In   breath-less si - lence kneel, With

trem-bling rap-ture feel The   hour of grace is   nigh;

Watch for the sig - nal given, As   for a voice from

Rallentando.   CHORUS *slow and*

Heaven, The   Lord is stand-ing   by.   Hush!

majestic.

Hush! Break not the spell! Je-sus is here; our hearts know it

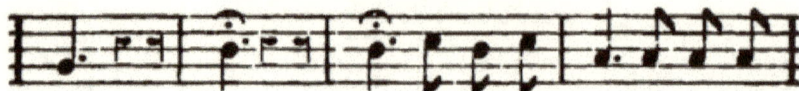

well.　　Kneel,　　Kneel! in love and fear; Je‑sus is

God and Je ‑ sus is　　here. Hark to　　the

P. (One voice.)

sound of the Sanc ‑ tu ‑ ary　bell, Tell ‑ ing of

F. (All.)　　　　P. (One voice.)　　F. (All.)

love, burn‑ing for　ev ‑ er, For　ev ‑ er,　for

P. (One voice.)　　F. (All.)

ev ‑ er! Tell ‑ ing of　love, burn ‑ ing for

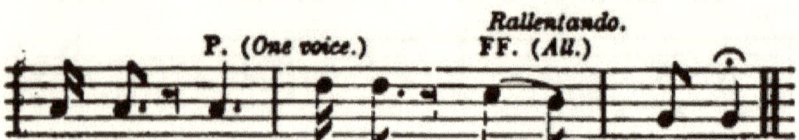

Rallentando.
P. (One voice.)　FF. (All.)

ev ‑ er, For　ev ‑ er,　for　ev ‑ er.

23.   'O what Wonders of Love.'

SOLO. Moderato.

Oh   what   won-ders of   love   on   the

al - tar   I   see, From the   Host, our dear   Lord is

look-ing on   me ;   He looks on the   crea-ture He

died   to   re - deem;   How   great is His   love, how

CHORUS.

small must mine seem !   O   dear - est   Lord ! teach me to

love   As do   the   Saints in heav'n a - bove.   O dear-est

Lord! teach me to   love As do the   Saints in heav'n a - bove.

---

24   'My God, my Life, my Love.'

Tune No. 60.

25. *Bread of Life.*

Tunes No. 102 and 80.

---

26. *The Altar.*

Soft and Slow.

O hap-py Flowers! O hap-py Flowers! How qui-et-

ly for hours and hours, In dead of night, In cheer-ful

p

day, Close to my own dear Lord you stay, Un-til you

f

gent-ly fade a-way! O hap-py Flowers! what would I

give, In your sweet place all day to

live, And then to die, my ser-vice o'er,

Rallentando.

Soft - ly as you do at His door.

27. *Thanksgiving after Communion.*

Moderato.

What hap - pi - ness can e-qual mine? I've found the

ob - ject of my love; my Sa-viour and my Lord di-

vine Is come to me from heav'n a - bove.

He makes my heart His own a - bode, His flesh be-

comes my dai - ly bread, He pours on me His heal - ing

blood, And with His life my soul is fed.

28. *Visit to the Blessed Sacrament.*

Cantabile.

Be - fore the al - tar An - gels vail their

fa - ces, For God is dwell-ing there by night and

day; His Heart is full of love, His Hands of

gra - ces, With which He crowns the souls that come to

pray. To His pre-sence re - turn-ing, With our

hearts bright-ly burn - ing, We come to

kneel be - fore His sa - cred feet, To see His

face and hear His words so   sweet. To see   His

face and hear His words so   sweet.

THE SACRED HEART.

29.   O Sacred Heart!

Slow.

Oh Sa - cred   Heart, Our home lies deep in

Thee. On   earth Thou art   an   ex - ile's rest, In

heav'n the glo - ry   of the Blest, Oh! sa - cred   Heart.

---

30.   To Christ, the Prince of Peace.

Tune No. 60.

31. *The True Shepherd.*

I was wan-dering and wea-ry, When my
Sa - viour came un - to me; For the ways of sin grew
drea-ry, And the world had ceased to woo me, And I
thought I heard Him say, As He came a - long His
way, O sil - ly souls! come near me; My sheep should
nev - ver fear me; I am I
am the Shep - - - - herd true.

32. *Jesus, the very thought of Thee.*

CHORUS. *Moderato.*

Je - sus! the ve - ry thought of Thee With

sweet - ness fills my breast; But sweet - er far Thy

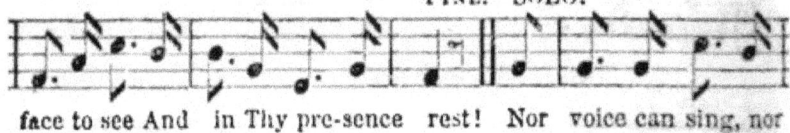

face to see And in Thy pre-sence rest! Nor voice can sing, nor

heart can frame, Nor can the mem-ory find, A

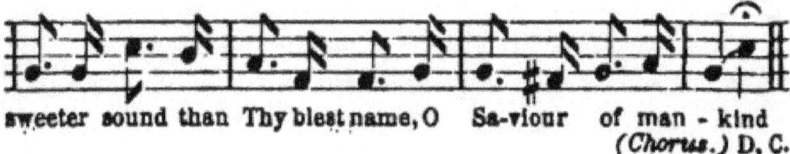

sweeter sound than Thy blest name, O Sa-viour of man - kind
(*Chorus.*) D. C.

---

33. *Evening Hymn to Jesus.*

Moderato.

Hear Thy chil - dren, gen - tle Je - sus,

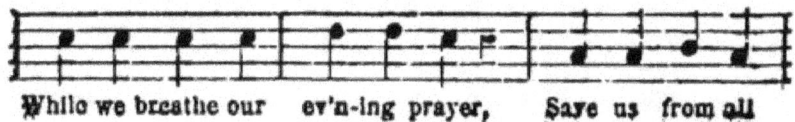

While we breathe our ev'n-ing prayer, Save us from all

harm and dan - ger, Take us 'neath Thy shelt r-ing care.

III. THE BLESSED VIRGIN MARY.

34. *St. Casimir's Hymn.*

H. E. C. W.

Sing, sing, each day, A tune - ful lay, My

soul, to Ma - ry's glo - ry: Her feasts em-ploy With

pi - ous joy To con her won - drous sto - ry.

---

35. *The Immaculate Conception.*

Moderato. SOLO.

"And can it be that God should

deign Like men to be of Sin - ners

born, From those on whom His curse hath

lain   The crea - tures of   a   world for-

CHORUS. *With spirit.*

lorn?   Our God   is   great, our God is high—yes

High!   His praise is   heard a - bove   the

sky! Nor may there aught of   sin   draw nigh—not

nigh!   To   where His   sov' - reign

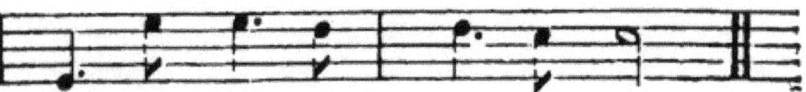

might, His sov' - reign   might doth   lie.

---

36.   '*O purest of Creatures !*'

Tune No. 63.

37. *Immaculate! Immaculate!*

SOLO. *Moderato.*

O Mo-ther! I could weep for mirth, Joy fills my heart so fast; My soul to-day is heav'n on earth, O could the trans-port

CHORUS.

last! I think of thee, and what thou art, Thy ma - jes - ty, thy state; And I keep sing - ing in my heart, im - ma - cu - late! Im - ma - cu - late.

38. *The Nativity of the Blessed Virgin.*

Tune No. 46.

39. *Our Lady's Expectation.*

Like the dawn-ing of the morn - ing On the

moun - tain's gold - en heights, Like the break-ing of the

moon beams On the   om of clou - dy nights, Like a

se - cret told by   An - gels Get - ting

known up - on the   earth, Is the Mo-ther's Ex - pect -

ta - tion Of Mes   -   si - ah's spee - dy   birth.

---

40. *The Sorrows of the B. V. M.*

Tune No. 99.

---

41. *The Assumption.*

Allegro.

Sing, sing ye   An-gel Bands, All beau - ti - ful and

bright; For   high - er still, and   high-er

Through fields of star-ry light, Ma-ry, your Queen, as-

cends, Like the sweet moon at night.

42. *The Triumph of the Blessed Virgin.*

CHORUS. F. *With Spirit.*

Queen of the skies tri - um - phant Queen,

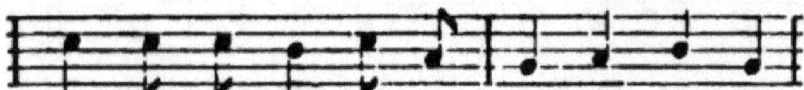

Each clime and age a glad tri-bute yield-ing

To thee their crown'd triumphant Queen, With heart and voice in glad

FINE. SOLO. P. *Soft.*

ac-cents sing. Love shall still in - spire, Hearts with sa-cred fire,

Love shall still in - spire Hymns of praise to thee, And our voi-ces

nev - er tire, While we sing with tune-ful glee.
(*Chorus*) D. C.

43. *Hail, Queen of Heaven.*

Hail! Queen of Heav'n, the O - cean star,

Guide of the wan - d'rer here be - low! Thrown

on life's surge we claim Thy care, Save us from

pe - ril and from woe. Mo-ther of Christ, Star of the

sea, Pray for the wan-der-er, pray for me.

---

44. *Daily, daily sing to Mary.*

Dai - ly! dai - ly, sing to Ma - ry, Sing, my

soul, her prai-ses due; All her feasts, her ac - tions

wor-ship, With the   heart's de - vo - tion   true. Lost   in

won-d'ring con - tem - pla - tion, Be   her   ma-jes-ty con-

fest; Call   her   Mo - ther, call   her

Vir - gin, Hap - py   Mo - ther, Vir - gin   blest.

45. *The Praises of Mary.*

SOLO. *Adagio.*

Ho - ly   Queen we bend be - fore thee, Queen of

pu - ri - ty di - vine! Make us   love thee, we im -

CHORUS.

plore thee, Make us   tru ly to be   thine. Teach, oh

teach us, Ho - ly   Mo-ther, How to   con-quer ev' - ry

sin, How to love and help each

o - ther; How the prize of life to win.

46. *Look down, O Mother Mary.*

CHORUS.

Look down, O Mo - ther Ma - ry! From

thy bright throne a - bove; Cast down up - on thy

FINE. SOLO.

chil-dren, One on - ly glance of love. And

if a heart so ten-der With pi - ty flows not

o'er, Then turn a - way, O Mo - ther, And

Chorus.

look on us no more.

47. *Mother of Mercy.*

Mo - ther of Mer - cy day by day My
love for thee grows more and more, Thy gifts are strewn upon my way Like sands up-on the great sea shore. Like
sands up - on the great sea shore.

48. *The Sailor's Hymn.*

SOLO. *Moderato.* P.

Ma - ry Mo - ther! Shield us through
life! Pro - tect us from The o - cean's strife;
CHORUS. F.
Calm the wild sea, Bid tem-pests cease,

Through thee we reach The shore in peace.

Through thee we reach The shore in peace.

49. *Mother Mary.*

SOLO. P. *Easy and flowing.*

I shall see this che-rished Mo-ther, This sweet

hope beats in my heart; Who can tell her love and

good-ness? In her pre - sence griefs de - part.

CHORUS. F.

Mo-ther Ma - ry, This dark night Is lit from

Hea-ven, With thy light. Mo - ther Ma ry,

This dark night Is lit from Hea-ven With thy light.

50. Consecration to the Blessed Virgin Mary.

SOLO *Moderato.*

I hear thy false sweet voice de - ceit-ful world, Vain are thy

lures and vain thy art - ful charms;

True to my Queen I own no rule but hers; My

hope, my home, is in my mo - ther's arms; Her badge I

wear, I own her sway, I fear no

CHORUS. *With ani-*

foes on the bat - tle day. Queen of the

mation.

sky, Mo-ther blest and be - loved, Turn on us thine

eyes, see we has - ten to thee, Lo at thy

feet, O dear Mo-ther we swear, True chil - dren of

Ma - ry for ev - er to be, True chil-dren of

Ma - ry for ev - er to be, True chil-dren of

Ma - ry for ev - er to be.

---

51. *To our Blessed Lady, for the Souls in Purgatory.*

Andante.

O turn to Je - sus, Mo-ther, turn, And call Him

by His ten-d'rest names; Pray for the ho - ly

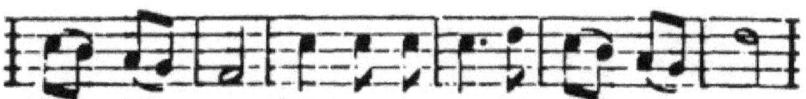

souls that burn This hour a - mid the cleans - ing flames.

Ah! they have fought a gal-lant fight; In death's cold

arms they per-se-vered; And af-ter life's un-chee-ry

night, The har-bour of their rest is neared.

52. Evening Hymn to our Blessed Lady.

Adagio.

Bright Queen of Hea-ven, Vir-gin most

fair, Ma-ry most gen-tle, List to our prayer,

Mo-ther, pro-tect us, Aid to us bring;

Sweet-ly en-fold us 'Neath shel-t'ring wing.

HOLY FAMILY HYMNS.

IV. ST. JOSEPH.

53. Hail! holy Joseph.

Tune No. 93.

54. Patronage of St. Joseph.

Cantabile.

There are ma-ny saints a-bove, Who love us with true love, Ma-ny Au-gels ev-er nigh; But Jo-seph! none there be, O none that love like thee. Dear-est of saints be near us when we die.

Rall.

55. *St. Joseph to the Infant Jesus.*

SOLO. *Moderato.*

Je - sus! let me call Thee son, Since

Thou dost call me fa - ther, How I

love Thee, sweet - est One! My God and son to-

CHORUS.

geth-er. Bless - ed St. Jo-seph to thee do we pray,

Of - fer our hearts to thy Je - sus to - day.

Of - fer our hearts to thy Je - sus to - day.

V. THE HOLY FAMILY.

56. *'Praise to Jesus, Joseph, Mary.'*

SOLO. *Moderato.*

Praise, praise to Je - sus, Jo - seph, Ma - ry, The three on

earth most like the Three in heaven!

Praise, praise to Je - sus, Jo - seph, Ma - ry, To

whom these Heaven-ly Likenesses were given! Come chris-tians,

come, sweet an - thems weav-ing, Come, young and

CHORUS.

old, come gay or griev-ing! Come christians, come, sweet anthems

weav-ing Come, young and old, come gay or

griev-ing! Praise, praise with me A - dor-ing and be -

liev-ing God's Fam - i - ly, God's Ho - ly Fam - i -

ly. God's Fam - i - ly, God's Ho - ly Fam - i - ly.

57. *The Banner of the Holy Family.*

CHORUS. *Vivace.*

Let us fight! for God let us fight! Come let us

throng round our Ban - ner! Wave it

high now our glo-rious ban - ner; See

how it glis-tens in the light: O Heart of

Jo-seph! O Heart of Ma-ry! Whose Heart with yours shines out so

bright? It is our Je-sus! It is our Sa-viour! Our

FINE. SOLO.

Lord, our lead - er in the fight! Hark! the

sound of the fight hath gone   forth   And we

must not tar-ry at home, For our Lord from the South and the

North, Has com - mand - ed his sol - diers to   come.
Chorus.

58. *Brightly gleams our Banner!*

Allegro.

Bright-ly gleams our Ban - ner, Point-ing to   the
FINE.

sky, Wav - ing wan-d'rers on-wards To their   home on high.

Hail, O ho - ly Ban-ner, Glad-ly   thus   we   pray;
D C.

And with hearts u - ni - ted, Take our heav'n-ward way.

59. *'Happy we who thus united.'*

Hap-py we who thus u-ni-ted Join in cheerful

mel-o-dy, Prais-ing Je-sus, Ma-ry, Joseph, In the Ho-ly

CHORUS.

Fa - mi-ly. Je-sus, Ma-ry, Jo-seph, help us,

That we ev-er true may be, To the pro-mi-

ses that bind us to the Ho-ly Fa - mi-ly.

---

60. *One Heart, one Soul have Brothers.*

CHORUS. *Cheerfully.*

One Heart, one Soul, have Bro-thers, By

love's e-ter-nal might, Of all and each they're

lov - ers, Who　walk in　hea - ven's　sight.　O

sweet the tie of　Brother. In　ho-ly bondage　bound,　As

sons of one same　Mo-ther In　true af-fec-tion found.

61. *All for Jesus, Mary, and Joseph.*

Let　those who seek the　world　to please, Do

all for hon-our, wealth, and ease; But　in the　Ho - ly

Fa - mi - ly, A　no - bler mo - tive,　far,　have we.

Liv - ing we will say, Joy - ful - ly each day, All　for

Je-sus, Ma-ry, Jo-seph! Dy-ing, we will cry,

Till our lat-est sigh, All for Je-sus, Ma-ry, Jo-seph.

VI. THE ANGELS AND SAINTS.

62. *Dear Angel ever at my side.*

Tune No. I.

63. *Saint Anne.*

Andante.

O Anne! thou hadst lived through those long dreary

years, When child-less-ness hung o'er thy home like a blight! But

An-gels, dear Mo-ther! were count-ing thy tears, And thy

patience, like Job's, had been dear in God's sight.

64. *Spotless Anna! Juda's Glory!*

CHORUS. F, *With Spirit.*

Gather'd round thy   sacred banner,   In the Church that

bears thy   name,*   Ma - ry's Mo - ther!   Gra-cious   An - na!

FINE.   SOLO. P.

We thy grace and   fa - vour   claim.   Spot-less An - na!

Ju-da's glory! Through the Church from   east to   west.

Ev - 'ry tongue   pro   -   claims thy   prai - ses,

CHORUS.

Ho - ly   Ma - ry's   Mo - ther   blest.

65.   *Saint Patrick.*

Tune No. 68.

* In churches not dedicated to St. Anne.

Here in homage of thy name

66. *St. Vincent of Paul.*

Tune No. 64.

---

67. *To St. Alphonsus.*

Tunes No. 39 and 44.

---

68. *Saint Aloysius Gonzaga.*

SOLO. *Cheerfully.*

An - gel - ic youth at whose blest birth Bright

Choirs of heav'n - ly spi - rits throng'd; How

great the day which gave to earth A

CHORUS. F.

trea-sure that to heav'n be - long'd. Pa - tron of

Youth! who pure hast known The dan-gers that be - set our

way,   We   fear   the   world   to

walk   a - lone,   Let   thy sweet name sup-port and

stay. Let thy   sweet   name sup-port and   stay.

69. *The Apostles.*

Tune No. 93.

---

70. *A Martyr or Confessor.*

Tune No. 47.

---

71. *A Virgin or Virgins.*

Tune No. 47.

---

72. *All Saints.*

Tune No. 47.

73. *All Saints' Day.*

Vivace.

Hail Feast of deep ce - les - tial joy,

Link-ing earth with Heav'n, Hap - py Saints en -

wreath'd with light, Stream - ing from God's

bless - ed sight, Praise to you be given.

VII. THE CHURCH.

74. *The Pillar of Truth.*

Tune No. 91.

---

75. *The Church.*

SOLO. *Tempo di Marcia.*

Who is she that stands tri - um - phant, Rock in

strength, up - on   the   Rock. Like some ci - ty crowned with

. tur-rets,   Brav - ing storm, and earthquake shock?   Who is

she her arms ex - tend-ing In bless-ing o'er a world re -

stor'd;   All the   an - thems of   cre - a - tion

CHORUS. F.

Lift - ing to cre - a - tion's   Lord?   Hers the

King-dom, hers   the   Scep - tre! Kneel, ye

na-tions, at   her   feet! Hers that Truth whose fruit is

Free - dom; Light her   yoke; her bur - then

sweet! Hers that Truth whose fruit is

Free-dom; Light her yoke; her bur - den sweet!

76. *The Holy Roman Church.*

Firmly.

I'll nev-er for-sake thee, I nev-er will

be, O Church of the Saints, an a - pos-tate from thee, Though

friends may en - tice me, and for-tune may frown, My

Faith and my Church un-til death I will own. My

Faith and my Church un-til death I will own.

77. England's Conversion.

SOLO. *Solemn.*

England! Oh, what means this sigh-ing From those

heaps of mos - sy stone; As of

spi - rits Mu - sic try - ing On some

harp, left crushed and lone? Through car - ved

shaft of aisles de - sert - ed, Bree-zes mur-mur still the

song, Which in ca - dence sweet con —

cert - ed Rais'd once there the cloister'd throng. Which in

ca-dence sweet con - cert - ed Rais'd once there the cloister'd

CHORUS. F. *With Spirit.*

throng. Ho - ly House - hold of sweet Na - za-

reth, Jesus, Ma - ry, Jo - seph! down

On each ser - vant ' look, who ga - ther - eth

Flowers for England's future crown; Hill, plain, valley, gar - den,

heath, Yield your bloom for England's wreath!

78. *Faith of our Fathers.*

SOLO.

Faith of our Fa - thers! liv - ing still, In

spite of dun - geon, fire, and sword. Oh,

how our hearts beat high with joy When - e'er we hear that

CHORUS.

glo - rious word; Faith of our Fa-thers! Ho - ly Faith!

We will be true to thee till death. Faith of our Fathers!

Ho-ly Faith! We will be true to thee till death.

VIII. THE CHRISTIAN LIFE.

79. *Young Men's Hymn.*

Tune No. 75.

80. *A Young Man's Colloquy with Jesus.*

Cantabile.

How sweet and pure Thy call di - vine That claims my

youth - ful heart, It tells me I may still be Thine And

see Thee as Thou art: It makes me long for joys un -

known, And sigh to burst life's ties; One

end in life it makes me own And count all other

lies. One end in life it makes me

own And count all other lies.

81. *Salvation.*

SOLO. *Moderato.*

Strive ye sal-va-tion to at-tain, 'Tis easy to a

will-ing mind, To ev-'ry Chris-tian, high-est gain,

Seek then, pur-sue it till ye find.

Seek then, pur - sue it till ye find.

CHORUS. F. *Firmly.*

Un - less sal - va - tion Un - less sal - va - tion

we ob - tain, All trea-sures of earth are

vain, All trea-sures of earth are vain.

82. *The Four Great Truths.*

The Solo and Chorus are sung to the same melody.

There is one true and on - ly God, Our

Maker and our Lord: And He Cre - a - ted

ev - 'ry thing By His Al - migh-ty Word.

83. *The Ten Commandments.*

Tune No. 82.

---

84. *The Seven Sacraments.*

Tune No. 82.

---

85. *I nothing fear with Jesus at my side.*

With animation.

To win my heart with visions bright and fair,

In vain the world with all its craft has tried:

F. *With energy.*

Harmless and weak its dazzling weapons are, I nothing

fear, I nothing fear, with Jesus at my side, I no-thing

fear, I nothing fear, with Je-sus at my side.

86. *The Vanity of the World.*

Adagio.

All things on earth are vain, Short lived and full of pain, Though hid-den in ap-pa-rent glee By the vain world propos'd to me, All this brilliant dis-play This vain show! The pride of a day! All must go: It fades from the sight, For oh! 'tis as fleet-ing as bright.

---

87. *Fight for Sion.*

CHORUS.

Christians! to the war! Ga-ther from a - far! Hark!

hark ! the word is given ; Je - sus bids us fight " For

God and the right." And for Ma-ry the Queen of Heav'n !

FINE. SOLO.

And for Ma - ry, the Queen of Heav'n ! Now

first for thee, thou wicked world ! Puff'd up with godless pomp and

pageant A - veng·ing grace to hum-ble thee Can

D. C.

make the weak - est arm its a - gent.

5

88. *The Christian Soldier.*

SOLO. *With decision.*

Oh! God of armies, hear our vow And make our pur - pose strong, We vow to fight for Thee till death, Our hearts to Thee be - long: We'll ne-ver yield our souls to sin, Nor do the tempter's will, We'd ra - ther die and for - feit all, If . we may love Thee still.

CHORUS. *With* Then Warriors

much animation.

on. come bat-tle for the Lord, Re -

solv'd to fight, and nev - er sheathe the sword Till

God shall call us to our home a - bove, And

fill us with per - pe - tual peace and love, And

Rallentando.

fill us with per - pe - tual peace and love.

---

89. *The Christian's Song on his March to Heaven.*

SOLO.

Blest is the Faith, di - ' vine and

strong, Of thanks and praise an end-less foun-

tain, Whose life is one per-pe-tual song,

High up the Saviour's ho-ly moun - tain.

CHORUS.

O Si-on's songs are sweet to sing With me-lo-

dies of glad-ness la-den; Hark! how the harps of

an-gels ring, Hail, Son of Man! Hail, Mo-ther-

p   <   *Rallentando.*

Maiden! Hail, Son of Man! Hail, Mother - Maid - en.

90. *The Pilgrims of the Night.*

SOLO.

Hark! hark! my soul! an - gel - ic songs are

swell - ing O'er earth's green fields and

ocean's wave-beat shore! How sweet the truth, those

bless-ed strains are tell - ing, Of that new life when

CHORUS.

sin shall be no more! An - gels of Je - sus!

An - gels of light! Sing-ing to wel - come The

pil - grims of the night, Sing - ing to

wel - come The pil - grims of the night.

91. *The Wounded Heart.*

Adagio.

The wound-ed heart loves on and weeps, And
ne - ver doubts its Fa - ther's care: But soft - ly to the
cross it creeps, And finds its watch-ful Mo - ther there. It
ne - ver doubts in cold dismay, Nor turns re-bel - lious
'neath the rod, But e - ver-more, by night and day,
Knows that its sor - rows come from God.

————

92. *For a Happy Death.*

Tune No. 101.

IX. MISSIONS AND RETREATS.

93. *Hail, Holy Mission, Hail!*

Slow.

Hail, holy Mission, hail! Sighing we turn to thee, For weary have we found The path of sin to be.

---

94. *On Death.*

CHORUS. F. *Grave.*

On to death, on to death We are hur-ry-ing fast: This hour, nay this mo-ment May be the last.

FINE. SOLO.

We all must dis, our doom is fixed, Nor youth, nor strength, nor art can save, As sure as now we tread _ the

D. C.

earth, So sure we're hast'ning to the grave.

95. *The Sinner conscience-stricken.*

Andante.

A - las! What grief and care My heart-strings

tear, And tears my cheeks be - dew! A - las! What

grief and care My heart-strings tear, With dread well-nigh despair—

'Twas not so When Thy ways were new; Oh Lord, no! For

I call'd Thee true. A - las! Vows made in

vain! Days full of pain! Can peace be mine a - gain?

96. *God and the Sinner.*

Adagio

O Sin - ner come un - to thy God, nor

la - ter De - lay to bend to God thy re - bel

knee; A - gainst His law too long thou'st been a

trai - tor, Re - turn to Him since He re - turns to

thee. Re - turn to Him since He re-turns to thee.

97. *The Wages of Sin.*

SOLO. *Andante.*

O what are the wages of sin, The

end of the race we have run? We have

slav'd for the mas-ter we chose, And what is the prize

CHORUS.

we have won? We are worn out and wea-ry with

sin; Its pleasures are poor at the

best; From what we re - mem-ber, not worth Half an

hour of a con - science at rest.

98. *Hymn of Repentant Sorrow.*

Andante.

Je-sus, my God, be - hold at length the

time, When I re - solve to turn a - way from

crime, O par-don me Je - sus, Thy

mer-cy I im - plore, I will nev-er more of-fend Thee,

Rallentando.

no, never never more. no, ne-ver more.

99. *Act of Contrition.*

SOLO. *Andante.*

God of mer-cy and com - pas - sion! Look with

pi - ty up - on me! Fa - ther! let me call Thee

Fa - ther! 'Tis Thy child re - turns to Thee!

CHORUS.

Je - sus! Lord! I ask for mer - cy, Let me

not im-plore in vain! All my sins—I now de-

test them, Ne-ver will I sin a - gain,

100. *The Triumphs of Grace.*

SOLO. *Cantabile.*

Joy, joy to the choir ce - les-tial, When a

soul is re-stor'd to grace, God owns a new throue tar -

res - tri - al, When weak man in truth seeks His

face— Joy, joy to the par - don'd sin - ner, Whom

God in His mer-cy hath blest; With His love a - bove all

o - ther And the pro-mise of end-less rest. And the

CHORUS.

promise of endless rest. Sing-ing praise to our God, Sing-ing

praise to His grace, We'll seek, we'll seek, the path his saints

trod, We'll seek, we'll seek, His will to em - brace.

X. THE HEREAFTER.

101. *Purgatory.*

Grave.

Bu - ried deep in   flames we   lie,

Pa-tient-ly we   weep and sigh, Far from God we

wait   in   pain, Till our souls are   pure a - gain. A -

las! A - las!   All the tears which   we   can   shed,

Can - not quench our   fie - ry   bed.

102. *Heaven.*

SOLO. *Adagio.*

Oh Heav'n! ce - les-tial   home!   Oh

bound-less land of love, I long to en - ter

thee And see my God a - bove.

CHORUS.

When will the An - gels come And

call my soul a - way? This

earth is dark as night, But

Rallentando.

Heav'n is bright as day.

103. *" Heaven is the prize."*

SOLO. *Moderato.*

Yes, Hea - ven is the prize My

soul shall strive to gain, One glimpse of par - a -

CHORUS.

dise Re - pays a life of pain. 'Tis

Heaven!—'tis Heaven!—yes, Hea-ven is the prize! 'Tis

Heaven!—'tis Heaven!—yes, Hea-ven is the prize.

CONCLUSION.

104. *Christ's Soldiers Rise.*

Tune No. 48.

LATIN HYMNS

AND TRANSLATIONS.

(A)   105.   *Veni Creator.*

Ve - ni Cre - á - tor   Spí - ri - tus, Men-
Come, - O Cre - a - tor,   Spi - rit blest! And

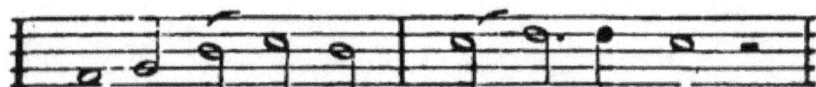

tes tu - ó - rum   ví - si - ta,
in our souls take   up Thy rest;

Im - ple su - pér - na   grá - ti - a. Quæ
Come, with Thy grace and   heav'n - ly aid, To

tu cre - á - sti   pé - cto - ra.   A - men.
fill the hearts which Thou   hast made.

(B)   106.   *Come, O Creator, Spirit.*

Andante.

Come, O Cre - a - tor, Spi - rit blest! And in our

souls take up Thy rest; Come, with Thy grace and heav'n-ly

aid, To   fill   the   hearts which Thou hast   made.

_____

(C) 107.   *Veni, Sancte Spiritus.*

Ve - ni Sancte   Spí - ri - tua,   Et e - mít- te
Ho-ly Spi-rit!   Lord   of Light! From the clear ce-

cœ - li - tus   Lu-cis tu - æ   rá - di - um.
les - tial height Thy pure beam-ing   ra - diance give.

Ve - ni, Pa - ter   páu - pe - rum, Ve - ni, da - tor
Come, Thou Fa - ther   of   the poor, Come with treasures

mú - ne - rum. Ve - ni, lu - men   cor - di - um.
which endure! Come Thou light of   all   that live!

_____

(D) 116.   *O Godhead hid.*

Soft and slow.

O   God - head   hid,   de - vout-ly I a -

dore Thee, Who tru – ly art with - in the form be –

fore me; To . Thee my heart I

bow with bend – ed knee, As fail - ing

quite in con - tem - pla - ting Thee. As fail - ing

quite in con – tem - pla - ting Thee.

(E) 117. *Lauda Sion.*

Lau - da Si - on, Sal - va - tó - rem,

Lau - da Du - cem et Pas - tó - rem,

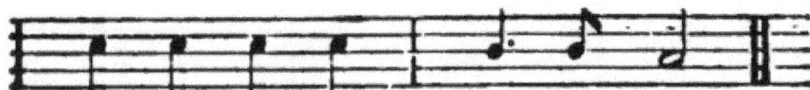

In hym - nis   et   cán - ti - cis.

The 21st and 23 verses begin thus:

Ec - ce,   Ec - ce.   Ec - ce   Pa - nis, &c.
Bo - ne   Pas - tor,   Bo - ne . Pas - tor, &c

(F)   121. *Pange Lingua.*

Pan - ge   lin - gua   glo - ri -   si

. Cor - po - ris   my - . ste - ri - um, . San - gui -

nis - que   pre - ti - o - si,   Quem   in

mun - di   pre - ti - um   Fruc - tus

ven - tris   ge - ne - ro - si   Rex   ef -

fu - dit gen - ti - um. A - men.

(G) 125. *Alma Redemptoris Mater.*

SOLO.

Al - ma, al - ma, al - - - -

- - - ma Re-demp-to-ris Ma - ter, quæ

per - vi - a cœ - li Por - ta ma - nes, et

stel - la ma - ris, suc - cur - re ca -

CHORUS.

den - ti. Por - ta ma-nes, et Stel - la ma - ris,

suc - cur - re ca - den - ti.

(H)   129.   *Regina cœli.*

FIRST SOLO. *Andante.*

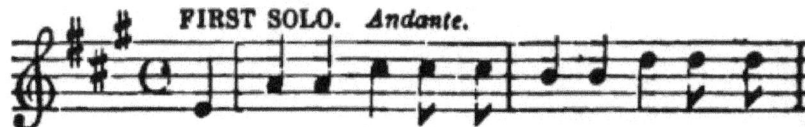

Re - gi - na cœ - li, Re - gi - na cœ - li, læ -

CHORUS.

ta - - - - re!   al - le - lu - ia, al - le -

lu - ia, al - - - le - lu - ia.

SECOND SOLO.

Qui - a quem me - ru - is - ti por - ta - re;

quem me - ru - is - ti por - ta - re; *(Chorus.)*

THIRD SOLO.

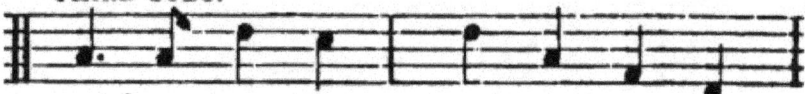

Re - sur - re - xit   si - cut di - xit;

Re - sur - re - xit   si - cut di - xit; *(Chorus.)*

FOURTH SOLO.

O - ra, o - ra, o - ra pro no - bis De-um; *(Chorus.)*

(I) 133. *Ave Maris Stella.*

A - ve ma - ris stel -

- la, De - i Ma - ter

Al - - - - ma, At - que sem - per

vir - - - - - - -go, Fe -

lix cœ - li por - ta. A - men.

(J) 141. *Miserere.*

Mi - se - rere me - i, De -

us: Secundum magnam mi - se - ri cor - di - am tu - am.

PRINTED BY RICHARDSON AND SON, DERBY.

ARCHCONFRATERNITY
OF THE HOLY FAMILY.

I. PRAYERS.—II. FEASTS,—III. INDULGENCES.

(Extracted from approved sources.)

I. PRAYERS

FOR THE MEETINGS OF THE HOLY FAMILY.

BEFORE THE CONFERENCE.

Invocation of the Patrons.

V. Pray for us, O Holy Patrons of our Association.
R. That we may be made worthy of the promises of Christ.

LET US PRAY.

O God! who dost assign to us each year some of the heavenly citizens for our Patrons; grant, we beseech Thee, through the intercession of those whom this year we have received as Patrons, that we, and all our relations, friends, and enemies, may presently experience the assistance of Thy grace: so that by the help of this same grace we may be enabled to practise those virtues which they have taught us by their example.

May all Thy Saints, O Lord, we beseech Thee, help us in every place, that while we celebrate their merits we may experience their protection. Through Christ our Lord. Amen

The Litany of the Holy Family.

Lord have mercy on us. ℞ *Lord have mercy on us.*

Christ have mercy on us. *Christ have mercy on us.*

Lord have mercy on us. *Lord have mercy on us.*

Christ hear us. *Christ graciously hear us.*

God the Father, of Heaven,

God the Son, Redeemer of the World,

God the Holy Ghost,

Holy Trinity one God,

Have mercy on us.

Jesus, Mary, and Joseph,

Jesus, Mary, and Joseph, worthy objects of our reverence and love,

Jesus, Mary, and Joseph, by the voice of all ages called the Holy Family,

Jesus, Mary, and Joseph, names for ever blessed, of the father, the Mother, and the Child, who compose the Holy Family,

Jesus, Mary, and Joseph, image on earth of the august Trinity,

Holy Family, tried by the greatest contradictions,

Holy Family, afflicted in your journey to Bethlehem,

Holy Family, rejected by all, and obliged to take refuge in a stable,

Holy Family, saluted by the Concerts of the Angels,

Have pity on us.

Holy Family, visited by the poor Shepherds,

Holy Family, venerated by the Wise Men,

Holy Family, persecuted and exiled in a strange country,

Holy Family, hidden and unknown at Nazareth,

Holy Family, model of Christian families,

Holy Family, living in peace and charity,

Holy Family, whose Head is a model of paternal vigilance,

Holy Family, whose Spouse is a model of maternal care,

Holy Family, whose Child is a model of obedience and filial piety,

Holy Family, who led a poor, laborious, and penitent life,

Holy Family, poor in the goods of the world, but rich in the goods of heaven,

Holy Family, despised by the world, but great before God,

Holy Family, our support in life, our hope in death,

Holy Family, patrons and protectors of our Confraternity,

Jesus, Mary, and Joseph,

Have pity on us.

Lamb of God, who takest away the sins of the world,

  Spare us, O Lord.

Lamb of God, who takest away the sins of the world,

  Hear us, O Lord.

Lamb of God, who takest away the sins of the world,

Have mercy on us.

Christ hear us, *Christ graciously hear us.*

LET US PRAY.

O God of goodness and mercy, who hast been pleased to call us to this Confraternity of the Holy Family, grant that we may always honor and imitate Jesus, Mary, and Joseph, so that pleasing them on earth, we may enjoy their presence in heaven. Through the same Jesus Christ, our Lord. Amen.

Memorare to the Blessed Virgin Mary.

Remember, O most pious Virgin Mary, that it has never been heard of in any age, that any one having recourse to thy protection, imploring thy aid, and seeking thy intercession, was abandoned by thee: I, therefore, animated with this confidence, O Virgin of Virgins, my Mother Mary, come to thee, and groaning under the weight of my miseries, cast myself at thy sacred feet. O Mother of the Word Incarnate, despise not my prayer, but graciously hear and grant my petition.

Memorare to St. Joseph.

Remember, O most amiable, most benevolent, most kind and most merciful father St. Joseph, that the great Saint Teresa assures us, that she never had recourse to thy protection withou obtaining relief. Animated with the same con.

fidence, O dear St. Joseph, I come to thee, and groaning under the heavy burden of my many sins, I prostrate myself at thy feet. O most compassionate father, do not, I beseech thee, reject my poor and miserable prayers, but graciously hear and grant my petition. Amen.

AFTER THE CONFERENCE.

The Examination of Conscience.

Let us examine our consciences, that we may see the faults we have committed this day, and let us ask pardon for them from God with our whole hearts.

The Spiritual Communion.

Come, Lord Jesus, I love Thee, I desire Thee; come into my heart, I attach myself, I unite myself to Thee. Let me never more be separated from Thee. *(St. Alphonsus.)*

Invocation of Jesus, Mary, and Joseph.

Jesus, Mary, and Joseph, I give you my heart and my soul.

Jesus, Mary, and Joseph, assist me in my last agony.

Jesus, Mary, and Joseph, may I breathe out my soul in peace with you.

SOLEMN ACT OF CONSECRATION.

O Jesus, Mary, and Joseph! I (*N*............)
in the presence of all the court of heaven—choose
you—on this day—for my patrons and protectors;
—I offer you—and solemnly consecrate to you—
in this Association—*my body,—my soul,—all that
I have,—and all that I am ;*—I promise you—to
live as a good Christian—that I may die—the
death of the elect—What a happiness for me—
to pass one day—from the arms of Jesus, Mary,
and Joseph,—in this world—into the arms of the
Father—the Son—and Holy Ghost in Heaven—
and that for all eternity:—such is my hope.—
Amen.

II. FEASTS

OF THE CONFRATERNITY OF THE HOLY FAMILY.

JANUARY.
   6. The Epiphany.

FEBRUARY.
   2. The Purification of the Blessed Virgin Mary.

MARCH.
   18. St. Gabriel the Archangel.
   19. St. Joseph.

APRIL.
   5. St. Juliana of Cornillon.
   — Sunday which follows the 7th of April.
   23. April.
   4th Sunday—The Flight into Egypt.

MAY.
   The Month of Mary.

JUNE.
   29. SS Peter and Paul.

JULY.
 1st Sunday.—The Feast-day of the Holy Family.
 3rd Sunday—The most Holy Redeemer.
 26. St. Anne.

AUGUST.
 2. St. Alphonsus.
 15. The Assumption of the Blessed Virgin.
 Sunday within the Octave : St. Joachim.
 Sunday after the Octave: The most holy and immaculate heart
  of Mary.

SEPTEMBER.
 8. The Nativity of the Blessed Virgin.
 14. The Exaltation of the Cross.
 3rd Sunday. The Seven Dolours of the Blessed Virgin.
 29. St. Michael, Archangel.

OCTOBER.
 2. The Holy Guardian Angels.

NOVEMBER.
 1. All Saints.
 2. All Souls.

DECEMBER.
 8. The Immaculate Conception of the Blessed Virgin.
 25. Christmas.

MOVEABLE FEASTS.

The Compassion of the B. Virgin.   Friday after Passion Sunday.)
Easter Sunday.
The Patronage of St. Joseph.   (3rd Sunday after Easter.)
Ascension Day.
Whit-Monday. (Feast of the Foundation of the Association.)
Corpus Christi.
The Sacred Heart of Jesus. (Friday after the Octave of Corpus
 Christi.)
The Feast of the Patron Saint of the place where the Confraternity is
 established.
The Feast of the Patron Saint of each Section. (For each Section.)
The Feast of the annual Patron of each Member.

III. INDULGENCES.

A *Plenary Indulgence* is granted by His Holiness Pius the Ninth on all the *Feasts* of the Archconfraternity of the Holy Family.

Also, I. On the day of the Solemn Consecration of the Members of the Holy Family.

II. On the day of the Procession of the Blessed Sacrament, for those who accompany it.

III. At the hour of death.

OBSERVATIONS.

1. Conditions to gain these Indulgences.—1st. Be enrolled a member of the Holy Family: 2nd, have received the Sacraments of Penance and the holy Eucharist. 3rd Recite some prayers (viz. 5 Paters and Aves, &c.) for the intention of the Pope in the Church of the Association.

2. When the Festivals fall on work-days, the Indulgence may be gained on the *following Sunday*.

Members prevented by sickness may gain the Indulgences without fulfilling all the above conditions.

3. These Indulgences may be applied to the souls of Purgatory.

An Indulgence of *one hundred days* is gained for :

1 Assisting at the Meetings of the Holy Family.
2. For the performance of many good works practised in the Confraternity.